LeaderTalk

LeaderTalk

Michaelene Grassli

BOOKCRAFT

Salt Lake City, Utah

Library of Congress Catalog Card Number: 96-84359
ISBN 1-57008-236-7

First Printing, 1996

Printed in the United States of America

Contents

Introduction

Let's talk leadertalk. It's a unique language. It's for anyone who has responsibility for influencing the spiritual development of someone else in a particular way. Whether you're a teacher, a member of an auxiliary presidency, a board member, a visiting teacher, or a committee chair or member, you are a leader. And parents are most certainly leaders! Learning the leadertalk language is essential for all of us.

I'm impressed with the number of faithful women in the Church today and their commitment to our loving Shepherd, the Lord Jesus Christ. This book is for those who have accepted the invitation to serve as his undershepherds through a Church calling.

The trust the Lord places in us to share in his redeeming work can seem overwhelming. Ammon said, "I am nothing; as to my strength I am weak" (Alma 26:12), and he acknowledged that only in the strength of God can any of us accomplish what he has asked us to do. It is with deep gratitude that I acknowledge the guidance of the Holy Ghost in my thirty-plus years of leadership experience, "for the Spirit speaketh the truth. . . . Wherefore, these things are manifested unto us plainly." (Jacob 4:13.) I also recognize the nurturing influence of the gifted women and men with whom I have served and from whom I have learned. Much of what you read here I learned under their influence, which cannot be overestimated.

The Church handbooks and manuals have been priceless as training tools and leadership textbooks during my leadership experience, and they continue to be my prime source of information regarding my current responsibilities. I turn to them over and over and learn from them much as I do the scriptures. You will notice that I refer many times to using the handbook for your particular calling.

I subscribe to the idea that to *do* good, we need to try our best to *be* good. Such qualities as basic integrity, loving the Lord and our brothers and sisters in the Church, and trusting others to do the best they can are essential to successfully helping people achieve their potential in our Heavenly Father's kingdom.

While my philosophy of leadership is based on this foundation, I have included in this book a rather practical side of the subject as well. We need to know some ways to function in the everyday tasks of leading—techniques, skills, and methods that can help us be effective and avoid exhausting ourselves in frustration, guilt, and failure. Many of us struggle unnecessarily, when utilizing a few principles and skills could make the way much more efficient and productive and more in harmony with the Savior's way of solving problems.

That's what this book is about—some simple principles and skills that can help make your leadership experiences productive and satisfying. While some of the examples are specific, the general principles are applicable to nearly any calling. I believe if principles are true, they are true in many applications.

I have tried to be as accurate as possible when describing Church procedures and representing policy and doctrine. But please recognize that I have not presumed to write as a representative of the Church. I simply have given my own perspective on what I have observed and learned in the hope that sharing the harvest of my years of seasoning might somehow strengthen others.

This book, then, is my offering to you. Enjoy learning from it and let it help you be the leader you want to be.

CHAPTER ONE

———————— ✀ ————————

You—the Leader

For God hath not given us the spirit of fear; but of power,
and of love, and of a sound mind.
—2 Timothy 1:7

When I was called as stake Primary president at what I then considered to be much too young an age, I cried for two days because I was so frightened of the new responsibility. I had served in presidencies with the young women for about eight years, with a one-and-a-half-year interlude teaching Primary. I really didn't know very much about the Primary program.

Fear is a common response to a new calling. Fear even causes some people to decline serving. But as Paul wrote to Timothy, fear is not of God. Instead, his gifts of power, love, and sound minds are strengths on which we can draw for courage to go forward.

What helped most in the beginning was my mother's counsel. I had my first taste of what principle-based leadership was when she advised me comfortingly, "Honey, what you have learned as a leader of young women is just what you need to be Primary president. You will just learn some new vocabulary."

And she was right. I studied the Primary handbook thoroughly—I even took it on vacation! And I learned the new vocabulary. Yes, I survived, with the aid of the handbook, prayer, lots of help from others, experience, trial and error, common sense, making do, and trying to listen for and act upon the promptings of the Spirit.

You can survive too! In fact, you can do more than survive. You can *thrive* as a leader.

What Is a Leader?

Have you ever been in a group—maybe a committee with an assignment—when nobody took charge to get something accomplished?

To be a leader, you must lead. Leaders are out in front, setting the pace and showing the way. Leaders get problems solved as they help others learn and grow. They don't do it alone, but their leadership sets the climate in which others serve and the standard others will strive for.

Some people are born leaders. They have always been leaders because they seem to be able to rally people to action.

A little girl I once knew, Sherry, at age nine organized her classmates and gave a surprise going-away party for her fourth-grade teacher, who was retiring. The party was complete with speeches, a skit, props, gifts, and refreshments. The following summer she enlisted her sister's help, and together they organized a backyard fair for all the children in her neighborhood.

Some people are like that. They can see what needs to be done. They get other people interested, everyone helps, and they all do good things.

Other leaders are quieter, but they come into leadership roles because their values, personalities, and styles cause others to trust them and to want to follow them. They are humble in important ways, but they take responsibility for problem solving. They often are the people of whom it is said, "Some are born great, some achieve greatness, and some have greatness thrust upon [them]" (Shakespeare, *Twelfth Night* 2.5. 143–45).

These words make me think of the time when Elder Ezra Taft Benson was invited by United States President-elect Dwight D. Eisenhower to be a member of his cabinet. When Elder Benson demurred, President Eisenhower convinced him by appealing to his sense of loyalty and duty to his country, and to the need for spiritual leadership in the nation. He inferred that this great man's wisdom and goodness were needed in the nation's halls of leadership. Elder Benson was the kind of man the president trusted to advise him as he made decisions for his country. Elder Benson was a farm boy from Idaho who had greatness thrust upon him. (See Sheri L. Dew, *Ezra Taft Benson: A Biography* [Salt Lake City: Deseret Book Co., 1987], p. 255.)

Whether or not we are born leaders, sooner or later most of us in the Church lead someone sometime. When we think of our eventual state or condition, we know we all have the potential to be leaders in the eternities. This means we can be wonderful leaders now. It's there inside us just waiting to be developed.

Growing as a Leader

I wanted and expected to be a wife, mother, and homemaker. I have been able to do just that. But I also have learned about writing and directing plays, leading congregational singing, teaching boys (our children are all daughters), keeping minutes, conducting meetings, Scouting, making posters, giving other women lessons in their homes as a visiting teacher, giving talks, planning luncheons for over one hundred women, and cramming much, much more into a day than I ever thought I could do—all because of Church callings. And that was before I was called to the Primary General Board! It seems that all my life I've been called to do things I didn't know how to do. It's like always being in the middle of earning a post-graduate degree in Growing. You know what I mean.

The Lord knows us better than we do. We may not feel qualified for a calling in ways we think we should be, but he knows that either there is something we need to learn or we have something that's needed at the time. Probably both!

We grow into our callings.

When we accept opportunities to serve as they are offered to us, we are accepting opportunities to grow. President Ezra Taft Benson encouraged full involvement in the Church when he said, "Now is the time for all who claim membership in The Church of Jesus Christ of Latter-day Saints to stand firm and demonstrate their allegiance to the kingdom of God. It cannot be done as a critic or as an idle spectator on the sidelines." ("A Marvelous Work and a Wonder," *Ensign,* May 1980, p. 34.)

Leading is definitely a process of getting off the sidelines and into the action!

And while we develop as leaders, we help others develop as people. We don't *make* them be better. We love, teach gospel principles, and create an environment in which people can grow. When people accept and live gospel principles, they become better people.

One of the great awakenings of my leadership experiences was when I realized that there are many ways to do things right. We can teach people about principles, then let them do things in ways that will fit them best, rather than imposing our particular style on them. When I learned as a leader to listen to the people I was leading and to differentiate between principle and style, I was more accepting of their ideas, and the end results were incredibly more productive.

So, regardless of my doubts about my qualifications to be a leader, somehow the Lord trusts me to assist in his work, because he has inspired leaders to call me to serve. And he is helping me grow as a leader.

And he trusts you.

That is why you have been called. And he will help you grow as a leader. It *is* a sacred trust. His work is more than just conducting a meeting or setting up chairs or making telephone calls. "For behold, this is my work and my glory—to bring to pass the immortality and eternal life of man" (Moses 1:39). That is what the meetings and telephone calls and setting up the chairs are all about—your eternal life and the eternal life of your brothers and sisters.

If Heavenly Father trusts you, then you can trust him, and you can trust yourself. Whether or not you are a born leader, the Lord will compensate for what you don't have. As Moroni said, "Yea, come unto Christ, and be perfected in him . . . then is his grace sufficient for you, that by his grace ye may be perfect in Christ" (Moroni 10:32). I believe this means, among other things, that today in your responsibilities he will enlarge what you do have, enabling you to accomplish well what he has called you to do.

And because of that, you—yes, you!—can be an effective leader.

CHAPTER TWO

The Best of All Leaders

For I have given you an example,
that ye should do as I have done to you.
—John 13:15

To be the best leader you can be, you can learn from the greatest leader who ever lived.

The earthly ministry of the Savior, our exemplar in all things, gives us a pattern of personal qualities of leadership. Some of his qualities we have naturally; others will need some developing. As we develop these characteristics we will improve our leadership, because we will be better people.

Consider four ways Jesus Christ was a leader and how you might learn from his example.

The Savior Loved Everyone

Just as he loved all men, women, and children regardless of their stations in life, Jesus taught us to do the same. Love, after all, is the first and greatest commandment. Our capacity for love is different from the divine capacity of Jesus Christ, which is rooted in his intimate knowledge of each of us, but his example of love is one we can follow. We can love all our brothers and sisters.

Elder M. Russell Ballard said, "Leadership based on love brings incredible power. It is real, and it generates lasting results in the lives of our Father's children." ("Strength in Counsel," *Ensign,* November 1993, p. 78.) We can love our families, our neighbors, and our associates in the Church in an upwardly spiraling cycle: Love motivates us to serve them, in serving we learn more about them, our love for them increases, and increased love, again, creates greater motivation to serve.

That reminds me of Twinkie. I had never liked cats much. They seemed to have an attitude problem. "You folks are so lucky to have me around," they seemed to be communicating. Not at all like friendly dogs who leap and pant with joy when they see you, and who seem to say only, "Love me! Love me!"

So it was not surprising that when neighbor children appeared at our front door with a box of kittens, one of which our children could choose for their own—for free!—I was not particularly interested. But when our five-year-old, who had been afraid of any living thing since a neighbor dog had knocked her over when she was three, pleaded with me to let her choose one, I couldn't resist. If a kitten would help her overcome her fear of animals, I would be brave and put up with the kitten—which would eventually become (ugh!) a *cat!*

We hadn't had the kitten, whom we named Twinkie, more than a week when my husband, Leonard, began painting our carport. Someone put the kitten on the fender of the car, and she slid off into the bucket of paint. She went all the way in. Totally covered.

Suddenly I cared about that cat. We moved into action. Leonard snatched her out as fast as he could, but she spit, bit, clawed, and writhed, frightening the children and making it impossible to hold her. We had to wrap a thick towel around her to be able to control her. Then we mopped and rubbed her and even poured paint thinner on her to try to get her clean.

We couldn't get all the paint off, so I called the family who owned the mother cat to see if our baby could come spend the night. I hoped the mother cat would finish the cleaning job. Mother cat and baby were locked in a shed together overnight. In the morning the kitten looked no cleaner, and our friends told us the mother would have nothing to do with her baby. (Twinkie did smell like paint thinner!) My heart went out to the poor little thing. I worried about her as I cuddled, fed, and watched her, and one day I realized that I was in love! Eventually the paint wore off, and Twinkie remained a treasured member of the family for ten years.

There is something about rescuing, caring, nursing, assisting, and working for others that generates love, even if someone is hard to love. Love makes us better people. Serving in the Church gives us opportunities to experience those feelings and become better.

Some Church members discovered this truth when their area was flooded with Asian refugees from several different countries. Local leaders couldn't seem to get the refugees who joined the Church integrated with the other refugees or with the established members.

Then someone thought of a possible solution. They mixed everybody up. They assigned home teachers and visiting teachers from the various groups to members in other groups. When they had ward, branch, or stake functions, committees included members from all groups. They tried every way they could to put the people together serving each other in cross-cultural groups.

It worked. Although it took some time for the members to get to know each other, learn to communicate, and establish relationships, when they worked together and tried to help each other, bonds began to form. It will be a continuing challenge, because people change slowly. But by caring for each other and by loving the gospel, they have begun to develop love for and unity with each other. As the Prophet Joseph

Smith said, "When persons manifest the least kindness and love to me, O what power it has over my mind, while the opposite course has a tendency to harrow up all the harsh feelings and depress the human mind" (*Teachings of the Prophet Joseph Smith,* comp. Joseph Fielding Smith [Salt Lake City: Deseret Book Co., 1976], p. 240).

As you pray for, teach, care for, and work for the members you have been called to serve, your love for them will increase. This seems to be an eternal natural law, because it always works, if we will let it. In serving others we are serving our Heavenly Father, the source of love. The Apostle John taught that when we love one another, we come to know God (see 1 John 4:7). When we know God, our capacity for love increases. As your love for your brothers and sisters increases, your effectiveness with and for them will increase. What a satisfying cycle!

Jesus Christ Sacrificed for Us

Jesus Christ made the supreme sacrifice of willingly atoning for our sins and giving his life that we might live again. We can follow his priceless example by being willing to serve and sacrifice for others.

Do the sacrifices required of leaders worry you?

Besides dealing with family responsibilities, most of us at some time in our lives face the pressures of disappointment, health and economic problems, personal tragedy, and heartbreak. Those are some very good reasons for sacrificing for the Lord, because sacrifice helps qualify us for the divine help we need to meet those challenges.

This reminds me of a definition of sacrifice I heard years ago: Sacrifice is giving up something you want now for something better later on. Now, I believe that sometimes you give up things that are *very* important today, and sometimes you can't see into eternity to realize what better things are to come—like giving up a little sleep (very important) to plan a lesson (that might save a soul). Sacrifice involves self-discipline, making hard choices (leaving the family and grandchildren to serve a mission, for example), and giving up personal comforts and desires for the benefit of others.

And yet, it seems to me that sacrifice, to be real, is giving up something with no thought of reward.

Some women decline to serve in responsible positions in the Church because they wrongly assume that to be successful in a Church calling means they risk being neglectful parents. Although the risk is there, wise leaders can rear their children responsibly while they give effective Church service. The service we give can be a demonstration to our children of our dedication both to them and to the Lord. It is one of those unspoken messages about the faith of a parent that children never forget.

My mother and father didn't preach to me about serving in the Church. They just did it. It was part of life. They seemed enthusiastic—happy about and interested in what they were doing—and if they ever complained, I didn't hear it. It was a priceless legacy for me.

Children also need to hear parents verbalizing how they feel about service. When I received the call to serve on the Primary General Board, our three daughters were ages four, nine, and eleven. I was fortunate to have been able to be at home with them during these young years. I'd had Church assignments to which I had given what I felt was considerable effort, but my prime concern, devotion, and time commitment were to my husband and our children.

So far my system had worked quite well, and I had been able to give what I thought was needed in both family and Church responsibilities. Leonard and I wanted to impress on the girls the significant message that in spite of the greater demands of this new call, it was important that I had accepted the invitation to serve.

We decided to tell the girls at dinner about the call that had come earlier that day. After the blessing on the food, we told them we had something important to tell them. We immediately had their attention. We reviewed for them past conversations about all of us having chosen in our pre-earth life to follow our Father in Heaven, about coming to earth, and about choosing to help his work grow while we are here. We talked about some of the callings Daddy and Mother had had, and how these were part of helping Heavenly Father. We talked about how good we felt about having been asked to help.

The girls were right with us. Our nine-year-old segued for us right into the next step by blurting, "What about kids? Kids should be able to help too! What can kids do?" What an opening!

From there we were able to tell them of my new call and explain that part of what children can do to help Heavenly Father is to help parents so they can fulfill their assignments. They were excited and felt involved in the decision to serve, as well as experiencing the personal desire to help Heavenly Father. Later, when we all discovered that there were some times I would be away from them, sometimes inconveniently, that commitment was already in place and the brief separations seemed to be acceptable.

I am grateful for the blessings given me when I've been set apart for various callings, because they have helped our children. One I remember specifically was when President Marian G. Romney set me apart as a counselor in the Primary General Presidency. He blessed our three daughters, two of whom were now teenagers, that my calling would be a blessing in their lives.

And it was.

One daughter tells of feeling warm and comforted when President Romney said those words. She said it was as if her Heavenly Father were telling her that yes, he did know her personally. The Spirit bore witness to her on that day that what she had been taught was true. She was indeed a daughter of a loving Father in Heaven who watched over her and was aware of her needs.

My feeling of sacrificing was lessened when I received a personal witness that my call to the general board was from my Father in Heaven. I was deeply concerned about being away from home at board meetings when the children returned from school. I now recognize that those times helped the children be independent and resourceful, but in the beginning it was of great concern to me.

One day I was contemplating this concern while in the temple. As we neared the end of the session, suddenly these words came into my mind: *You will know when your children need you.* A sense of relief washed over me. I completed the temple session comforted by the reassurance that I was doing what the Lord wanted me to do and that he was aware of me and my children. All would be well.

After that I didn't worry as much about being away from them on Primary assignments. I limited my absences the best I could. I tried to be the best mother I could be. I tried to be diligent in my duties, because I wanted that promise to be fulfilled. And it was. I seemed to sense when I needed to leave a meeting or ask to be excused from attending. However, I have not always been as sensitive to promptings as I should have been. I do have some regrets—after all, pain is part of progress. But all in all, the blessing has been fulfilled.

When I was president, the girls were into their adult years, in college, marrying and starting families. At this stage they all had some challenges regarding my calling. I was less available to help them than I would have liked to have been. They had to deal with my higher visibility and the accompanying assumptions and expectations that were placed on them by others. This sometimes was hard for them.

One daughter felt prompted—she says compelled by the Spirit—to attend a meeting in which I was speaking to Primary leaders. She recalls that during the talk she had a specific feeling of comfort envelop her. She realized that her sacrifice of not always having her mother available to her was important because Primary was important. When she was called as a counselor in her stake Primary two days later, it was made known to her that her call was because of her own qualifications and worthiness, not because of her mother.

Experiences such as these are verification to me that the Lord is more than fair. He expects us to serve, and he helps and blesses us and those around us when we do. Our service makes us worthy of his blessings, which, if we recognize them, bring us great joy.

Now, when we recognize our blessings, something very significant happens: *The service we give seems less of a sacrifice.* We aren't serving out of duty and counting the things we give up. We are serving mostly because we love to do it. It feels good. We want to keep doing what feels good. This is when we begin to understand the concept of true consecration. It ceases being a sacrifice because what we may give up seems unimportant when compared with the way we feel when we serve.

We are serving because we love the Lord.

The Savior Led with Patience

An examination of Jesus' parables shows that he taught what people were ready to receive and then let them progress at their own pace. The parables were simple stories to those who weren't ready to receive the deeper message: "Therefore speak I to them in parables: because they seeing see not; and hearing they hear not, neither do they understand" (Matthew 13:13). Those who did understand the message were blessed by the greater knowledge they received from the same stories.

Think of Jesus' patience with Peter. When Peter's faith failed him while walking on the Sea of Galilee, Jesus stretched forth his hand to the sinking Peter and reassured him that there was no need to doubt. When Peter, along with James and John, dozed in Gethsemane, Jesus apparently did not become angry. While acknowledging their weak spirits, he simply reiterated his request that they be watchful. As their leader, he did not give up on them. He helped Peter overcome weaknesses and grow into the responsibilities of chief Apostle. Peter later led the Church after Jesus' ascension.

The Savior's teachings of peace reveal his patience. He also said to seek after the one, to go the second mile, to turn the other cheek, and to forgive seventy times seven.

I am amazed at the patience the Lord had with the children of Israel while they were wandering in the wilderness. Time after time, even after witnessing and being the recipients of stunning miracles, they reverted back to their old habits of idolatry. Time after time, even though the Lord often had to "restrict their privileges," he gave them another chance.

I sense the Lord's patience with us today when I read, "Verily, verily, I say unto you, ye are little children, and ye have not as yet understood how great blessings the Father hath in his own hands and prepared for you; and ye cannot bear all things now; nevertheless, be of good cheer, for I will lead you along" (D&C 78:17–18).

As a leader, it is hard to be patient with others who don't do what you think they should. If teachers don't show up, or the bishopric doesn't fill a vacant position, or the visiting teaching hasn't improved, or the chairs haven't been set up, or the phone calls haven't been made, we could get angry and impatient. And probably no one would blame us. But the more mature and experienced we become as leaders, the more we understand that people grow in their time and according to their individual situations. Remembering the Savior's examples of patience can help us.

The Savior Had Confidence in What He Was Doing

The Savior knew the purpose of his mission. As a boy, when his parents found him teaching in the temple, he said, "Wist ye not that I must be about my Father's business?" (Luke 2:49.) His responses to Satan's efforts to tempt him show the understanding he had of his divinity and earthly mission.

Because he was certain of his direction, he taught with power and conviction and was not deterred by opposition. He did not hesitate to take action when it was needed, such as when he found it necessary to cleanse the temple.

Your leadership will be most effective when you, following the Savior's example, are confident of your direction and can move forward with assurance. This confidence can allow you to imagine what could be happening in the lives of the people you lead and to help instill that vision in others.

Be bold, resourceful, and creative. Follow the handbook as you find new ways to do things. Don't let the gap between what could be and what is discourage or frustrate you. Try to understand what is needed and how you can be part of the solutions, not part of the problems.

Confidence is rooted in testimony and faith in the Savior and in our ability to be sensitive to the promptings of the Spirit. We can continue to fill our reserves of faith and testimony through daily prayer and scripture study, obedience to the principles of the gospel, and loyalty to our general and local Church leaders. There are no shortcuts. The eternal patterns and requirements for revelation and inspiration are constant and reliable.

When we follow the Savior's example of love, sacrifice, patience, and confidence, we will lead in the way he would want his children led.

CHAPTER THREE

Principles of Presidency

For where two or three are gathered together in my name,
there am I in the midst of them.
—Matthew 18:20

Diane, a capable young mother, was called as Young Women president in her ward. She had a strong testimony, many ideas, and lots of energy. She served for a few months, wore herself out, and asked for a release. Her bishop had observed that she had tried to do nearly everything by herself. He met with her and helped her understand the concept of presidency and how she could multiply her own efforts by using her counselors effectively. This help was so valuable to her that she was able to continue as president for two more years.

The Concept

In a presidency—with a president and two counselors—no leader needs to function entirely alone. A presidency functioning unitedly gives the combined effect of their individual

testimonies, talents, and wisdom to any effort—and the syner-
getic result is much more than if each were functioning inde-
pendently. Brother Stephen R. Covey calls this *inter*dependence (see *Seven Habits of Highly Successful People* [New York:
Simon and Schuster, 1989], p. 185). When we understand the
strength in presidency, we can see why the Lord instituted
presidencies as the way Church leadership would be organized today. The pattern of presidency is rooted, I believe, in
the concept of counseling together that is taught in the scriptures: "The Gods took counsel among themselves" (Abraham
4:26).

It is my feeling that this concept of presidency has been
patterned for us by our Father in Heaven, by Jesus Christ in
his earthly ministry, and by leaders of his church anciently
and in modern times. For example, we can recognize a pattern
of presidency in the process of creation; in the leadership of
Peter, James, and John; and in the organization of priesthood
quorums during the Restoration period (see D&C 107).

In section 5 of the Doctrine and Covenants we can see an
illustration of the need for a leader to have help. The Lord told
Joseph Smith, "There are many that lie in wait to destroy thee"
(verse 33). He had told Joseph that he would call three witnesses as one way "that thy days may be prolonged" (verse
33). The men who would be witnesses would receive testimonies through the Spirit and be prepared to share the responsibility for declaring the Book of Mormon. Joseph must
have been grateful to have partners to sustain him and share
in the responsibility.

One of the blessings of having a presidency lead an auxiliary today is that each member of the presidency can be "pre-
served." In a presidency there is a balance of ideas, effort, and
responsibility. President Gordon B. Hinckley has taught, "Two
counselors, working with a president, preserve a wonderful
system of checks and balances" ("'In . . . Counsellors There Is
Safety,'" *Ensign,* November 1990, p. 50). With three people receiving inspiration and giving their best efforts, their decisions

will seldom be in error. "In the multitude of counsellors there is safety" (Proverbs 11:14). The combination of talents affords great strength to a presidency.

The President

The president presides. It is her responsibility to prayerfully seek the will of the Lord and to understand and follow handbook guidelines, policies, scriptures, and the counsel of priesthood leaders so that she will preside worthily. This will inspire in the counselors trust and confidence in her and in her decisions. As a counselor I found that it is easy to follow a president who is humble, obedient, and prayerful. With her foundation of knowledge, the president can help the counselors understand what they need to know, including their duties.

The president shares the burdens and blessings of leadership with the counselors by delegating assignments to them. Ruth Wright, who served with me as second counselor in the General Primary Presidency, considers delegation the most important skill for a president to develop and exercise. I can understand why. Because there are a great many things that only the president can do, it is important for her to give her counselors responsibility for nearly everything else. Even after delegating, the president ultimately bears the responsibility for all that is done.

Together, members of a presidency gather information and analyze problems. The president is ultimately responsible for the final decisions on matters the presidency members consider together, but she needs to seek for, listen to, and heed the wise counsel of the counselors. The three of them need to agree on most matters, and final decisions need to be unanimous.

The president can encourage the counselors to express their honest feelings by asking for their opinions without giving her own opinion first. She needs to respect their opinions and consider them carefully. When the counselors feel respect from their president, they will feel safe in expressing themselves freely.

I particularly like a description of the decision-making process given by Elder Richard G. Scott in a presentation to the General Authorities. He said, "I know that the [*General Handbook of Instructions*] indicates that 'after consultation and prayer, the stake president makes a decision and invites his counselors to sustain it.' However, it is my conviction that a presidency that has a pattern of open discussion with the intention of reaching a unanimous decision can be led by the Spirit to reach a united conclusion without the need for the president to use the unilateral power of decision granted to him." (General Authority Training, 8 April 1992.)

A wise auxiliary president will do what Elder Scott described President Howard W. Hunter as having done. "Once a group made a presentation to the Quorum of the Twelve regarding a proposed adjustment in Church procedure. They concluded and left. President Hunter then asked for an expression of feeling on the matter. During the discussion, one of the Twelve said, 'I don't know why, but I feel unsettled about this proposal.' Further discussion was delayed, with a decision to invite the group to make a more detailed presentation. That was done. President Hunter looked at that member of the Twelve, saw his furrowed brow, and without additional comment said, 'I see there is still some unsettled feeling about this matter. We will table it for future discussion.'" (Ibid.)

Unanimity in a presidency is strengthening and unifying. If one member is uncomfortable or uncertain about a matter, maybe it would be a good idea to do as President Hunter did in this instance and table the matter for consideration later. The president takes the lead either in moving forward with a matter or in deferring it for a later time.

The president needs to refrain from criticizing or complaining if a counselor is not functioning as the president thinks she should. Dwan Young, who preceded me as general Primary president, never showed her frustration with me, although I'm certain she would have been justified in doing otherwise. Instead, we'd chat about how my assignments were progressing. She would ask how she could help. We'd talk about whether presidency assignments needed to be re-aligned. These conversations gave me clues about ways I could improve, and they encouraged me in a positive way.

The Counselors

President Hinckley has taught priesthood leaders that counselors serve as assistants, partners, and friends to the president (see "'In . . . Counsellors There Is Safety,'" *Ensign,* November 1990, pp. 49–50). When the president nominates the women whom the bishopric or stake presidency will call to serve as her counselors, she needs to be prayerful and thoughtful as she considers whom to suggest. From the options available to her, she should try to select faithful women with whom she feels she can be compatible, because they will be working closely with one another. She needs to trust them and have confidence in their abilities. It is helpful if they have talents and strengths that complement her own, so that the combined presidency can have a broad range of attributes to draw upon as they lead.

You will notice that I refer to the counselors as *the* counselors rather than *the president's* or *her* counselors. That is intentional. I tried hard to remember to refrain from referring to the wonderful women who served as counselors with me as *my* counselors. The president does not own the counselors. Feelings of ownership of people, organizations, or programs are detrimental and should always be avoided. These feelings tend to generate pride and could lead to manipulating others or exercising autocratic power. Doctrine and Covenants 121 refers to this as "unrighteous dominion."

Counselors sit in council with the president. They need to be open and candid as they express their opinions and present information on the matters that are brought forward for consideration. If a counselor doesn't have an opinion on a matter, she may need some time for thought and consideration to formulate one. She needs to think creatively about the entire organization, beyond her own assignments. That is what the president needs from her. This is why she is a counselor.

One Young Women president wrote, "When I'm doing dishes, folding clothes, or taking a walk, I often assess how we are implementing the Young Women program in our ward. I try in these moments of reflection to sense where change or strengthening or better communication is needed. But I don't want the burden of doing this alone. I expect each counselor to be doing the same thing, not only for her own assignments but also for the whole program. If a counselor thinks only about her part, the organization may suffer from lack of her insight and gifts. After all, it is because of her gifts that Heavenly Father has placed her there."

Counselors need to fulfill their responsibilities as given in the handbook and as they receive assignments from the president. The president can authorize a counselor to represent her in conducting a meeting or attending a council when she is absent. Often a president hesitates to ask counselors to take assignments because she doesn't want to put undue strain on them. But she needs to have confidence in her counselors and to feel free to ask for their help. In addition, the counselors can make it easier for her to give them assignments when they offer. Then they need to fulfill the assignments willingly, giving their best efforts to be successful.

It is a great blessing to the president when counselors offer to take on an assignment. "I'll do that" or "Would you like me to take that?" were music to my ears. I had a major assignment one summer that would require me to be out of town for two weeks in the month prior to the wedding of one of our daughters. Just when I was feeling the pressure of not being ready for the wedding, one counselor offered to take my heavy out-of-town assignment. I gratefully accepted her offer!

A counselor needs to humbly assess her own gifts and decide how she can use them to help. One Relief Society counselor wrote to me, "I'm a good administrator, and I think I can help the president in this area without taking over or making her feel inadequate. At a Relief Society event, I was greeting the sisters as they arrived, but the president wasn't there. I found her in the kitchen dishing food instead of hosting, as a president needs to do. I changed places with her, explaining gently that the sisters needed their leader where they could see her."

In making decisions, the two counselors do not constitute a majority to outvote the president, but should instead try with the president to seek for unanimity in their decisions. This does not mean that they always have to have the same opinions on a matter. In fact, sometimes it is better if their opinions are very different, because it helps ensure that all possibilities are being considered.

We enjoyed some lively discussions in our general presidency meetings, where several points of view were often expressed. We laughed frequently about how we couldn't agree whether it was better for children to attend Primary at the beginning of Sunday meetings or at the end. It is possible to disagree without being disagreeable or contentious. You can differ with dignity. That is what I was fortunate to experience with counselors. You may want to talk together about trying to avoid hurting each other's feelings and about not allowing your feelings to be hurt. I believe that the stronger our testimonies are, the less likely we are to be offended.

I believe it is not necessarily a requirement of unity for one to change the opinions of the others, although that often happens. But each can sincerely try to be humble and to seek for the will of the Lord. In reflecting on how this works, Betty Jo N. Jepsen, who served with me as first counselor, told me, "Full submission of personal will to the Spirit of the Lord is essential." And she added, for those of us who are strong-willed, "This is hard!"

It is true—sometimes submitting to the will of the Lord is hard to achieve, but as the Lord said to Joseph Smith concerning the Three Witnesses, "I will give them power that they may behold and view these things as they are" (D&C 5:13). If all members of the presidency are humble, the Lord will help them know when a decision or course of action is correct. They all can then support the decision and feel peace concerning it.

Acting as the Lord's Servants

Whenever the presidency meets they need to remember that they are the Lord's representatives and servants. Because of this, they need to meet in the name of the Lord. They will want to call upon him in prayer, seeking the Spirit in all they do. The Lord tells us, "Put your trust in [my] Spirit. . . . I will impart unto you of my Spirit, which shall enlighten your mind, which shall fill your soul with joy." (D&C 11:12, 13.) The presidency can strive to know the Lord's will and to act according to the promptings they receive.

If the presidency study together the instructions from the handbook and the counsel from the Lord that is found in the scriptures, they will be guided to know what he would have them do, for the scriptures and the handbook will teach them the will of the Lord.

Loyalty

In order to reap the blessings of unity, the members of a presidency need to be loyal to each other. It would be contrary to principles of Church organization and to the principle of unity for counselors to speak against the president, or to teach or act in a way contrary to decisions they have made as a presidency. Counselors do not make major decisions without the president.

President Hinckley knew well the role of being a counselor. For many years he was a counselor to ailing presidents, carrying much responsibility for leading the Church—sometimes when the other counselor also was incapacitated by ill health. Of leading the Church as a counselor during these times, he said, "In matters where there was a well-established policy, we moved forward. But no new policy was announced or implemented, and no significant practice was altered without sitting down with President [Spencer W.] Kimball and laying the matter before him and receiving his full consent and full approval." ("'In . . . Counsellors There Is Safety,'" p. 50.) This is an example that counselors in auxiliary presidencies could reliably imitate.

The president can set the standard of loyalty. She too should be loyal to the counselors and to the decisions they make together. They are a team of three, and they need to function as a unified entity.

Business should be conducted and decisions should be made with both counselors involved. It is important for everyone to be informed and to contribute. If one counselor cannot attend a presidency meeting, it is my opinion that the president, if possible, needs to postpone the meeting until all can be there. One benefit of this is that both counselors will know they are needed and valued, which is important to their being able to help the president. It helps them feel responsible for being in attendance at meetings and for carrying their share of the responsibilities. When they realize business will not be conducted without them, they feel an obligation to be there.

Confidentiality

With the trust the Lord has given you comes the solemn obligation to maintain confidentiality concerning matters that are discussed in the presidency. For example, when you consider names of people to submit for new callings, their circumstances may need to be weighed in the process. There are times when priesthood leaders may discuss with you information about pending decisions. Such deliberations and others regarding the circumstances of members should be kept strictly confidential, because to do otherwise may prove hurtful or embarrassing to someone—even to you. It is a sacred trust to be an undershepherd, and the ability to keep confidences is a justification of that trust.

One bishop explained to me that he felt strongly about maintaining confidentiality. In fact, he told me that should he learn of a breach of confidentiality, he would feel that was just cause for releasing the leader who broke that trust. That is strong language, but it reflects the solemnity of the principle.

What if your presidency doesn't function quite as I have described? What? You are normal, imperfect people? How fortunate! That means you have the opportunity to practice gospel principles of love, patience, understanding, and loyalty. Sister Virginia H. Pearce has said, "The miracle of it all is that we *are* real people put into an ingenious structure [the organization of the Church], designed by God, to help us become like him" ("Ward and Branch Families: Part of Heavenly Father's Plan for Us," *Ensign,* November 1993, p. 81; emphasis in original). The ideas about presidency that I have outlined in this chapter do work, but not always without effort. Realistically, everyone is "in process," and you need to work patiently toward where you want to be.

And that's enough.

CHAPTER FOUR

Understanding Church Government

*The rights of the priesthood are inseparably connected
with the powers of heaven.*
—D&C 121:36

When I was general Primary president, an intelligent, faithful, and sincere stake Primary president visited me in my office one day. She had an idea about curriculum that she wanted to implement in her stake, but it was not finding fruitful ground with some of the stake and ward leaders. Her idea was a worthy one, and she had the best of intentions. Her purpose for meeting with me was to seek my approval for her plan. She thought if I liked it, I could give her permission to carry it out.

My desire was to be supportive, but I knew that I would not be true to principles of Church government if I did what she was asking. Instead, I explained that I could make some suggestions about how she might discuss her desires with her local leaders, but the approval for her plan needed to come from the priesthood leaders who had jurisdiction in her stake.

I tried to explain that the General Authorities would also respond to a stake president in much the same way. They encourage the local leaders to make the decisions.

Although the stake Primary president was very disappointed, I think she understood and could see the wisdom in the plan of Church government. I hoped our conversation helped her. She certainly helped me. Her feelings about Primary lessons helped confirm in my mind that our plans for revising the Primary curriculum—to be implemented about a year later—were indeed needed.

When leaders of faith and testimony understand and sustain the inspired system of Church government, they are able to work harmoniously within the system, and their lives and the results of their efforts are blessed. Without this understanding, they tend to become frustrated by their inaccurate perceptions and their unrealistic expectations, and they may attempt to circumvent established procedures.

Women Leaders and the Mission of the Church

The mission of the Church is to invite everyone to come to Christ. To do that, the Church focuses on missionary work, on helping members live the gospel of Christ and prepare for eternal life, and on family history and temple work. These three dimensions of the Church's mission are commonly referred to as "proclaiming the gospel," "perfecting the Saints," and "redeeming the dead." Everything we do as leaders needs to be based on this mission. You will notice that conference messages, lesson manuals, handbooks, and Church magazines all center on some aspect of helping people to share the gospel; understand, accept, and live the gospel of Jesus Christ; and enjoy the blessings of ordinances and covenants.

The Role of Women in Church Leadership

Besides giving spontaneous care in their families and to others in times of need, women leaders in the Church are authorized through callings inspired of God and issued by priesthood leaders to assist in an official way in the mission of the Church. As we function in our assigned Church duties, we discover that our Church work is to help prepare ourselves and others to receive the saving principles and ordinances of the gospel and to make and keep sacred covenants, that we might receive the fulness of the blessings our Father in Heaven has in store for us.

Women help administer the programs of the Church in wards and stakes. We preside over, direct, and staff auxiliaries. We teach, advise, observe, evaluate, and train. Auxiliary presidents are members of and participants in the priesthood councils. We represent the interests of the children, young women, and adult women of the Church as well as offering our specific insights into the implementation of the Church programs in the lives of all members. All leaders can receive the blessings of God in their lives and in their Church work. We are entitled to receive inspiration and guidance through the Holy Ghost.

There are many faithful, educated, talented, and influential women in the Church today. In addition, Church correlation, strengthened and refined in recent years, has helped bring into harmony all organizations and departments of the Church. This has the powerful potential of magnifying the influence of righteous and faithful Church women, because we are more unified with our brethren in purposes, programs, and efforts as we function to help accomplish the mission of the Church. And in that unity is strength.

Agency—Choice and Accountability

Central in the Lord's plan for our earthly experience is the pivotal and eternal principle of agency. We are free to choose and are responsible or accountable for the results of our choices.

In achieving the mission of the Church, leaders strive to follow the words of the Prophet Joseph Smith, who, when asked how he governed the Church, responded, "I teach them correct principles, and they govern themselves" (as quoted by John Taylor in "The Organization of the Church," *Millennial Star* 13 [15 November 1851], p. 339). The General Authorities and officers of the Church do everything they can to teach us and encourage us to be faithful. They "counsel Church members to depend first of all on themselves for decisions about the application of gospel principles. On the other hand, obedience—willing and energetic submission to the will of God even at personal sacrifice—is a central gospel tenet. Far from contradicting freedom, obedience is its highest expression." (*Encyclopedia of Mormonism,* s.v. "agency.") President Brigham Young taught that obedience "is the only way on the face of the earth for you and me to become free" (as quoted in ibid.).

Because of the desire of general Church leaders to hold fast to the principle of agency, there may be times when you will not receive the detailed directions you might wish to have. That is when you have the opportunity to go to your knees and seek for inspiration and direction to know what is best. And when directions are very specific, you can be assured they are important and need to be followed. As you develop as a leader, you too will want your decisions and actions to allow for the individual accountability of those with and for whom you serve.

The Priesthood

The Lord's house is a house of order. He gives the Church direction about accomplishing its mission in an orderly way— through the priesthood line of authority. The Lord reveals his will for the Church to his living prophet. We receive direction from the prophet and his counselors (the First Presidency) and the Quorum of the Twelve Apostles through other general and area authorities, through stake presidents, and then through bishops. This direction may come in conference messages, Church magazines, letters, bulletins, handbooks, and manuals from Church headquarters. We can depend on this orderly system of Church government, the priesthood line of authority, as being constant and reliable, because the Lord is directing it and he is unchanging—constant and reliable. We don't need to wonder what the Lord wants Church members to know. When the prophets speak, we know. That is how he governs his church. This does not preclude our receiving our own inspiration for the many aspects of our lives and Church responsibilities.

The highest intellectual and spiritual goal of both men and women in the Church is to become as God is. The Lord organized his church on earth for the purpose of helping all of God's children attain that eternal goal. He organized and governs his church by the power, authority, and presiding right of the eternal and everlasting priesthood.

All Church leaders function according to priesthood direction and principles as they invite others to come unto Christ and be exalted in him. President Spencer W. Kimball stated, "The Church does not have several organizational lines running from headquarters leaders to their local counterparts. There is only one fundamental organizational channel, and that is the priesthood channel." ("Living the Gospel in the Home," *Ensign,* May 1978, p. 101.)

It is my firm conviction and testimony that the teachings of the prophets regarding the priesthood system of Church government are correct. It is not a plan devised by men, but one revealed by God through his designated representatives—John the Baptist, Peter, James, and John. There are those who wonder why Latter-day Saint women are not ordained to the priesthood. There are three reasons why this issue doesn't bother me:

One, I trust the Lord and his living prophets. I have had the opportunity to work closely with many of the General Authorities. Utilizing the priesthood procedures outlined in the handbook, we met regularly with our advisers. We met with the Brethren in the councils and studied various matters with them in many meetings. These many years of experience have given me the greatest respect for the wonderful men who lead our church. Further, I know they are the Lord's servants. They have not been put in place by man, but by God. Regardless of their differing backgrounds, personalities, opinions, and talents, in the Lord's work and through the Holy Spirit they become unified for the good of the work. When a decision is made, they are one. Many times as I observed them I had the feeling come into my heart, *This is true. This is right.*

Second, I've seen the orderly functioning of the Church with men and women in their assigned roles. We can see that the Church certainly is flourishing under this system. Elder Neal A. Maxwell of the Quorum of the Twelve wrote:

> We know so little about the reasons for the division of duties between womanhood and manhood as well as between motherhood and priesthood. These were divinely determined in another time and another place. We are accustomed to focusing on the men of God because theirs is the priesthood and leadership line. But paralleling that authority line is a stream of righteous influence reflecting the remarkable women of God who have existed in all ages and dispensations, incuding our own. (In *Woman* [Salt Lake City: Deseret Book Co., 1979, p. 94.)

Third, there is no question in my mind that my earthly and eternal blessings are dependent upon whether I love God and obey his commandments, keep my covenants, and endure faithfully to the end. I do not need to be ordained to the priesthood to do these things. I know of no spiritual blessing of which I am or will be deprived because I do not bear the priesthood. I know that if we submit humbly to the will of our Father in Heaven and obey him and follow his prophets, we will be blessed with all the Father has for us. If there is more I should know, the Lord will reveal it in due time. The opportunities open to us now and eternally are limitless! That is certainly enough for me. There is peace in my heart concerning this matter.

Utilizing the Priesthood Line

Although the Church functions under priesthood leadership, all members have the same mission of teaching and strengthening each other. "This is not man's work nor women's work," noted Elder M. Russell Ballard. "It is *all* God's work." ("Strength in Counsel," *Ensign,* November 1993, p. 77; emphasis in original.) Because of that, women and men can be considered partners in the work of the Church.

General Authorities have used the word *partner* in describing the equal status of men and women in the Church. President Spencer W. Kimball "pointed out that women are 'full partners' with men" ("Privileges and Responsibilities of Sisters," *New Era,* January 1979, p. 42). John A. Widtsoe is quoted as saying, "In the Church of Christ woman is not an adjunct to but an equal partner with man" ("The 'Mormon' Women," *Relief Society Magazine,* June-July 1943, p. 373).

Elder Bruce R. McConkie emphasized the spiritual equality of men and women: "In all matters that pertain to godliness and holiness and which are brought to pass as a result of personal righteousness—in all these things men and women stand in the position of absolute equality before the Lord" ("Our Sisters from the Beginning," *Ensign,* January 1979, p. 61).

Understanding principles of Church government helps us to see our distinct leadership roles and to function effectively as a team. I grew up in the little town of Blackfoot, Idaho. We used to say that we had the widest main street in the world. And it probably is true. There is West Main and East Main, and right down the middle are several sets of railroad tracks. To go anywhere in the middle of town, we had to cross those tracks, and we often submitted to the temptation to try and walk the rails of the tracks.

If you have ever tried to walk railroad track rails, you know it is not an easy thing to do. The rails are fairly narrow, very smooth, and a little bit curved on top, and we found that we couldn't walk very far without falling off. We would compete with each other to see who could walk the farthest without falling.

Well, we found it was a lot more fun to stay on the tracks than to fall off. So we devised a way we could do that.

We stopped competing.

Instead, we would walk parallel to each other. When we were reaching out and touching hands to gently support one another, we could keep our balance and stay on. Then we could go as far on the tracks as we wanted.

I like to think about women leaders in the Church and their bishopric, high council, or stake presidency advisers in the same way. If they gently reach out and support one another—not compete, dominate, intimidate, or control, but effectively support—then they all can progress in their personal spirituality as well as accomplish the purposes of their callings.

In meeting with women leaders, I sometimes heard them say about a priesthood leader, "He doesn't support us very well." My response would usually be something like, "How do you support him?" In a partnership, each has a responsibility to fulfill his or her assignments in ways that sustain the other. Complaining or criticizing is an indication of nonsupport.

In the partnership of an auxiliary presidency and their bishopric, for example, I see two sets of responsibilities this way: One greases the wheels for the organization, and the other turns the wheels. I consider the bishopric, high council, or stake presidency advisers to be facilitators. They organize the auxiliaries and issue calls to serve. They set the meeting schedules, allocate budgets, and advise leaders. They "grease the wheels" so that auxiliaries can function. Presidencies and boards of the auxiliaries I consider to be implementors. They support priesthood leaders in implementing the mission of the Church, bringing the auxiliary programs to the members of their organization. They conduct auxiliary meetings, teach lessons, nurture, activate, and strengthen the members. They "turn the wheels" of their organization.

When each partner functions effectively in his or her particular role, then the members' lives can be blessed. They can go as far on the gospel track as they want.

Besides being accountable to her Father in Heaven, a ward auxiliary leader is also accountable to her bishopric regarding her organization. She needs to seek their counsel, direction, and approval on major decisions regarding her organization. They can teach, train, motivate, and inspire her. And she can be of great help to them.

The relationship of a ward auxiliary leader to her stake auxiliary leaders is different from her relationship with the bishopric. From both her bishop and her stake leaders she can receive training in the auxiliary program and policies as well as motivation and inspiration. However, because she is directly accountable to her bishopric through the priesthood line of authority, stake auxiliary leaders do not give permission, nor do they enforce policy.

Similarly, a stake auxiliary leader is accountable to her stake presidency. General presidencies and boards help set policies and procedures that are given in the handbooks, and they certainly can be called upon to explain, teach, motivate, and inspire. But they are not enforcers of rules or permission-givers.

When you understand the mission of the Church, the significance of the principle of agency, the role of the priesthood in governing the Church, your role as a leader, and how to utilize the priesthood line of authority, you understand some of the fundamentals of Church government. Such understanding can facilitate your ability to work under the influence of the Spirit of the Lord, and can have a profound, positive effect on the service you give in leadership.

CHAPTER FIVE

Participating in Councils

Let one speak at a time and let all listen unto his sayings,
that when all have spoken that all may be edified.
—D&C 88:122

The Lord has established quorums, presidencies, and councils to facilitate the governing of the Church. The importance of councils in this process has been emphasized by the General Authorities as they instruct stake leaders. "In these perilous times," said Elder M. Russell Ballard, "we need the cooperative effort of men and women officers in the Church, because absolute vigilance is required on the part of all who have been entrusted to help watch over the kingdom. We each have large individual responsibilities, but just as important is the responsibility we share with others to come together in council in a united effort to solve problems and bless all of our Church members." ("Strength in Counsel," *Ensign,* November 1993, p. 77.)

Councils allow leaders to come together to provide the collective resources of all to strengthen one another in their individual callings. Decisions are based on the group consensus of what they feel is right, rather than on what may be the opinion of the person of strongest will. In this sense councils can help prevent unrighteous dominion and serious error. Governing by council is taking the higher way, accomplishing good things with qualities identified by the Lord as essential to exercising righteous influence, such as persuasion, long-suffering, gentleness, and kindness, without hypocrisy and without guile (see D&C 121:41–42).

In order for a council to accomplish its important purposes, each member of the council needs to be committed to true principles and to the process of the council. Each needs trust in and respect for the others to be able to work together productively and righteously.

The most basic council in the Church is the family council, under the direction of parents. Here all members of the family can participate in establishing family goals, making family decisions, and learning about and living the gospel within the family.

A bishopric or quorum or auxiliary presidency, though not called a council, functions on the principles of a council. Ward councils, under the direction of bishops, provide an opportunity for priesthood and auxiliary leaders in attendance to counsel together and plan how to proclaim the gospel, perfect the Saints, and redeem the dead within the membership of the wards. Other Church councils include stake councils, stake high councils, and area councils, where decisions are made concerning the members within stakes or areas.

These councils are similar to those organized at general Church headquarters. The quorums of the Seventy, the Quorum of the Twelve Apostles, and the First Presidency all constitute councils. It is in these councils, and in other executive councils in which general leaders of auxiliaries participate, that decisions affecting the general membership of the Church are made.

In ward and stake councils, auxiliary presidents have the expanded opportunity to assist in planning for the blessing of Church members and nonmember neighbors. General Authorities have taught both women and priesthood leaders about how to make ward and stake councils function effectively, with all members of a council participating and contributing.

"All councils in the Church should encourage free and open discussion by conferring with one another and striving to have clear, concise communication," said Elder Ballard. "Councils should discuss objectives and concerns, with mutual understanding being the ultimate goal. . . . The primary focus . . . should be coordinating activities and stewardship. . . . Leaders should review together their responsibilities and find ways for Church programs to help members live the gospel in the home." ("Strength in Counsel," p. 76.)

Elder Ballard further suggested that council meetings be used "for finding answers to questions on how to improve sacrament meetings; how to improve reverence; how to focus on children [of course, I loved that one!]; how to strengthen youth; how to help singles, including single parents; how to teach and fellowship investigators and new members; how to improve gospel teaching; and many similar issues" (ibid., pp. 76–77).

During my tenure at Church headquarters, I learned of many examples of marvelous commitment and love among Primary leaders. One example is a fitting illustration of the potential of stake and ward councils. A new stake Primary president noticed that there were many children in the stake who didn't attend Church meetings. She took her concerns and a plan to her stake council, who concurred that something should be done.

The names of all nonattending children were put on index cards and distributed to the wards in which the children resided. The ward council in each ward organized a search for every child and recorded all known facts on the cards.

Where possible, the Relief Society and Melchizedek Priesthood quorums assigned the children's Primary teachers as visiting teachers and home teachers to the families of nonattending children in their classes. As the visits were made to the homes of the children, relationships were formed, and parents and children became friends with these Primary teachers, who were also involved in their work as priesthood holders and members of Relief Society.

Many positive things happened. The intent was to find the children who were not receiving the blessings of the gospel in their lives. In their search, these leaders discovered the temporal as well as spiritual needs of some of the children and their families.

One little girl, seven-year-old Jessica, was visited by the ward Primary president several times in her home. Jessica's mother had been a member of the Church for three years but was totally inactive. The Primary president told Jessica that she would like to have her come to Primary, and she described what they were going to be doing the next week. The following Sunday, when the Primary president saw Jessica and her mother appear in the doorway of Primary, she said, "Jessica, I'm so glad you could come!" Jessica said, "I pulled the covers off my mommy and told her we were going to Church!"

Other ward members, in searching for one child, found he had died, and his parents were sorely in need of comfort and support, which ward members were then able to give. These grieving parents would not have received such help if the ward council had not gone in search of the child.

After a year, an accounting showed that all but two children were located and contacted. Not all the children were activated, but blessings came into many lives, and attendance at Primary increased. An additional but unexpected result of this activation effort with the children was that attendance at Relief Society and priesthood meeting increased as well.

The search for the children began with the concern of one woman for the spiritual welfare of children she did not know but for whom she felt great love and responsibility. She enlisted the help of stake and ward councils, and the children became not just names on cards but individuals about whom someone cared.

Presidents of auxiliary organizations, and counselors who attend in the president's absence, need to be prepared to make such meaningful contributions in their ward and stake councils.

Ideas for Participating in Councils

The opportunity to gather information that will be useful and helpful in ministering to the needs of the members in your organization is an important benefit of participating in a ward or stake council. In order to do this it is important to listen to what transpires in the council meetings. You can gain an understanding of the purposes of the organizations of the Church, the goals of your leaders, and the concerns of other leaders for members. This can broaden your own store of information that can influence decisions you make and actions you will take. It is as important to listen in a council as it is to talk—maybe more!

One of the most valuable contributions leaders can make in a council is to give information, because the decisions made in councils are best when all pertinent information has been considered. A president needs to be aware of the welfare of the members of her organization—their feelings, needs, and circumstances. She needs to bring this information to the council. In addition, she needs to have with her, either in her head or on paper, the vital statistics of her organization; that is, information such as enrollment, attendance, nonattenders, baptisms, awards earned by members, members preparing to advance, visiting teaching information, and services given by and for members. She should be aware of the trends in these areas among the members of her organization so that action can be taken to encourage or deflect these trends as needed. The secretary of her organization can be responsible for accumulating and updating this information for her.

When the president has these kinds of information readily available to her, she will be prepared at any time to add to a discussion when such matters are under consideration. She can also raise questions and issues as she feels they are needed.

In addition, when matters are under consideration in the council, she can research an issue and report. In most discussions of the council she should feel free to give her candid opinions and observations on any matter. If her ideas are clearly expressed with an attitude of unity, humility, and help-fulness, she will be able to make a significant contribution.

It takes forethought, practice, and experience to contribute effectively in a group, so be patient as you develop your skills in this area. The Spirit can help you in your efforts and can en-hance and clarify in the minds of your listeners the righteous thoughts and ideas you wish to convey.

If you are a president, there may be a time when you are asked to make a presentation to your ward or stake council, or when you feel such a presentation is needed and you have asked for time on the agenda to do so. As you prayerfully pre-pare for such a presentation, these suggestions may be helpful:

1. Plan to be as brief and concise as possible while ade-quately covering the information and ideas you have. Find out how much time has been allotted to you, and *do not* go over that limit. Take less time, if possible.

2. Write down what you want the result of your presentation to be. What do you want your hearers to know or feel or do after they have heard you? This is your objective.

3. Outline the main points you wish to cover. As you plan, ask yourself, *Will this help me accomplish my objective?* Use only those ideas that will best make your point.

4. Plan how you will present your ideas. Your beginning needs to capture the attention of your listeners. Examples and stories illustrate your ideas and help lis-teners understand what you are trying to say. End your presentation with a summary statement or challenge that will let the council members know for certain what has been the purpose of your presentation. You may want to include your testimony.

5. Decide if a handout or overhead transparencies would help you drive your message home. If you use a hand-out, it's usually best if it is no longer than one side of one page.

6. Practice giving the presentation so that you will be secure with your words and visual aids and you will be able to adjust for time limits if you need to. Practice speaking clearly, looking directly at council members, and standing squarely on both feet without shifting your weight. When you speak clearly and with confidence, those present will likely be receptive to your message.

If the ward or stake council in which you participate does not operate quite like what I have described, be patient. Elder Ballard, as an adviser to Primary, Young Women, and Relief Society, generated chuckles and knowing nods when he told the women of the Church, "Be patient with the Brethren, and know that the General Authorities are teaching priesthood leaders in stakes and wards to listen to you and to counsel with you on matters pertaining to the needs of young and older women. Your opinions are valuable, even essential, to the Brethren because no one else has your perspective and insights. You have much to offer in strengthening the homes and families of the Church. We marvel at your strength, we value your service, and we rejoice in your faithful quest for eternal life." ("Be an Example of the Believers," *Ensign,* November 1991, p. 96.)

The council system has great potential for carrying on the Lord's work in the Church. Our individual effectiveness is increased many times when we work together cooperatively in councils.

CHAPTER SIX

Serving Together in Unity

*And he commanded them that there should be no
contention one with another, but that they should
look forward with one eye, . . . having their hearts
knit together in unity and in love
one towards another.*
—Mosiah 18:21

Why do some organizations within the Church—presidencies or committees—seem to be able to get many good things done and help other people effectively, while others can't seem to get much accomplished at all? One factor that might be considered is the presence or absence of unity; that is, harmony or oneness of mind and feeling.

The Lord said, "If ye are not one ye are not mine" (D&C 38:27). Since we need the Lord's blessings in all we do, unity is surely worth striving for. Unity in the Church is not necessarily being alike or agreeing on everything all the time, but it is agreeing on purpose, goals, or outcomes. When we serve together in the Church, the mission of the Church and the purposes of our organizations should form unifying foundations for what we do. Then, when we work together harmoniously, those purposes can be achieved. Elder M. Russell Ballard said, "When we act in a united effort, we create spiritual synergism, which is increased effectiveness or achievement as a result of combined action or cooperation, the result of which is greater than the sum of the individual parts" ("Strength in Counsel," *Ensign,* November 1993, p 77).

Then why would becoming united within our Church groups be difficult? Aren't people really very much alike? We all have dreams and goals and frustrations. We have the same desires to be happy and successful, to have productive and satisfying relationships with others, and to have peace in our lives. All of us have days filled with the challenging daily tasks of living.

We need many of the same things. We all need to feel that we are worthwhile people. We all need to know and love our Heavenly Father. Each of us needs to understand and follow the teachings of our Savior, Jesus Christ.

Yes, we are very much alike. But we also are different in many ways. We are different in appearance, intellect, experience, gender, education, and culture. Each of us has our own talents and interests. We vary in physical ability, spiritual development, and economic circumstances. We fill varying roles in our families, in society, and in our callings in the Church.

Some of those differences are thrust upon us without our having any vote in the matter. Some differences cause us to misunderstand each other and result in conflicts that make us frustrated and unhappy. Some of the most troublesome differences are often very superficial. Irritating mannerisms, eccentricities, personality quirks, and pet peeves can make us impatient, disgusted, even angry. Our differences can be deterrents to unity, unless we learn how to understand and manage them.

However, most of our differences—even if we don't like them—are results of the blessings of individual worth and uniqueness given to us by our Heavenly Father. They make our world and our lives interesting, and they enrich our relationships. Indeed, our differences can be a deciding factor in the success of our personal and group efforts.

For example, my life has been enriched because of my college roommates. One was a talented organist from New Jersey who played very serious classical music. One was from the very southern end of California, and cooked us Mexican food that I had never tasted before (I grew up in Idaho in the fifties, before ethnic foods were everywhere). One roommate was a girl who had graduated from high school a year early and was on an academic scholarship. Another was a sophisticated Northern Californian with elegant tastes. The other roommate was a raven-haired, blue-eyed beauty who majored in English and was a student officer.

I was a self-conscious small-town girl with what I considered no notable qualities. I was rather overwhelmed, even intimidated by their diverse backgrounds, personalities, and talents. I said so to my mother in a phone conversation one day, and her response surprised and motivated me: "Oh, honey! What an opportunity for you! Learn as much as you can from them."

And you know, I did, thanks to Mother's wise counsel.

From the organist I gained a familiarity with Bach, an appreciation for organs and organists, and an increased love of classical music. From the Southern Californian I learned to cook Mexican dishes that became staples in my future family's diet. From the young scholar I learned what studying really meant—I didn't achieve academically as she did, but I learned what it takes to excell. Being around the Northern Californian made me want to refine my manners. From the English major I received loyal friendship, inspiration and help with my writing, and the use of her typewriter. And most important, I met my husband through her.

As general Primary president, it would have been easiest for me to assemble a board constituted of women who were a lot like I am. But instead, our presidency and board were intentionally selected for their diversity, in addition to their gospel scholarship, talents, and experience. We had scriptorians, scholars, musicians, and writers. There were single and married women, creative minds and methodical ones, lifelong members and converts, women who were employed and those who were not, experienced Primary leaders and women who hadn't been in Primary for years, serious women and jolly ones. Their backgrounds, experiences, and personalities were widely varied.

All that diversity mixed up in the thirty women who served on our board made for a rich learning experience for all of us. We needed all of them in the work we did. We tried to let each one do what she did best, while at the same time giving them opportunities to grow in other areas of their lives too. We were able to accomplish much more because of their diversity than if we had all been stamped from the same mold.

Our challenge in leadership, then, is to make the most of our God-given differences—to form cohesive groups where all can find deep satisfaction and personal growth as we successfully strive to help others. Developing unity in a diverse group can be done with thought, planning, inspiration, and time. When people share experiences as they focus on and contribute to a common cause, struggle together to overcome difficulty, and share their testimonies with one another, they come to know and appreciate each other. Hearts seem to get knit together, inviting the Spirit to bless our efforts.

This is unity.

What follows are some ideas that can help foster unity within your organization.

Accept Others

A bookmark pinned to the lampshade on my desk reminds me that "God sees us as he would like us to be . . . but loves us as we are." Willingness and ability to accept and appreciate the individuality and diversity of those with whom you serve is a key to your success as an undershepherd. Each person has great value, is loved by Heavenly Father, and has potential to help achieve the purposes and goals of your group. If you can recognize these strengths, or accept that they exist even if you can't see them yet, you will be taking a giant step toward achieving unity.

A woman once told me, "My husband loves me in spite of my faults. And more than that, he told me he even loves me *because* of my faults!" I thought that was an interesting way to think about the marriage relationship, and about accepting one another in general.

Granted, we all have faults, but our job in life is to identify and correct our own faults, not those of others. One of the reasons our differences can inhibit unity is that sometimes we perceive a friend's, spouse's, or coworker's differences as faults. We see others as somehow inherently flawed when they do not believe or behave as we do. Differences are not faults. They are differences.

Remember that we were created to be different from one another. That diversity was intentional, so it must be good. The Savior sees us all as worthwhile regardless of our individual uniqueness. When we can accept one another, even if we do not always approve of others' behavior, we will make considerable progress toward achieving unity with one another.

Your example of accepting others will help those you lead become more accepting of others. You also can do some specific things to help others in this regard. There are activities that help people understand each other better and feel more connected to one another. Sometimes activities like these are called "boundary breakers." They do take time but are worth it.

Here is an example of such an activity: Give all members of the group a paper cup with the same number of M&Ms as there are members of the group. Each person takes a turn telling the group something about themselves that they think the others have not experienced. If any of the others have not had that experience, they give that person one M&M. The apparent object of the game is to get as many candies as you can.

The real object of the game is to learn about one another. Another version of this game is to tell things you think the others don't know about you.

Another example: Have members of the group fill out a brief questionnaire that includes questions such as: What is your favorite book of all time? What do you do if you don't have to do anything? What is the most important thing you have learned in the last year? What is the best advice you ever received? Have each member read their answers to each question aloud. Love and acceptance develop when we know each other's hearts.

Remember when you were a child and you quarreled with a sibling? Maybe your mother assigned the two of you to clean a window—one of you on the inside and one of you on the outside. You probably ended up grimacing at each other through the glass as you worked and laughing away your disagreement.

That principle can work for adults working together in a group. Some disagreements or hard feelings can be dispelled when the people involved are assigned to work closely for the benefit of someone else—or for each other. It shouldn't be busywork but a task or project of real substance. This works especially well with youth. As a leader, you can try it as a means of developing acceptance within your group. Be careful, however, not to create hostility by pushing togetherness on those with deeply held and emotional differences. Doing so could be counterproductive.

Nothing softens hearts and unifies like praying together. I was told about one president who felt contention and resistance from a counselor. One day she met with the counselor about a matter in their organization and suggested that they pray together about the matter. The president offered the prayer and included a heartfelt plea that the relationship between her and the counselors would be sweet, loving, and cooperative. With the counselor listening, the president prayed to be wise enough to refrain from doing anything that would alienate her friend, and she expressed her gratitude and love for this woman who served as a counselor in their organization. It was a way of expressing her sincere feelings in a non-threatening manner. This occasion was the beginning of a new page in their relationship, and they became close friends. Sincere prayer can invite the Spirit into a relationship and can result in increased love and understanding.

Avoid Criticizing Others

Many years ago I heard a speaker say that he thought there was no such thing as constructive criticism. I tend to agree. All criticism does is give vent to the criticizer's frustrations and pride. Criticizing is a quick path to hurt feelings, disunity, and even apostasy. If we truly accept others, we will not be inclined to criticize them. It is better for the soul and for our receptivity to the Spirit simply to refrain from being critical.

What if you're determined to not criticize and someone with you begins to be critical? Criticism is an easy trap to fall into. I have fallen into it many times. Maybe something that happened to me will give you an idea of something to try.

One occasion when I was on the Primary General Board, I began to make some critical comments, and the board member with me didn't respond to what I was saying. At first I took her silence to be sympathy, so I continued. Then, when I paused, she abruptly changed the subject. She was gentle about it, but there was no doubt in my mind that she didn't wish me to continue my tirade. It was a compelling lesson that remains vivid in my memory, and I have tried to do better since then.

On another occasion I was driving a carload of young women to camp when I overheard some of the girls begin to make uncomplimentary remarks about a leader in the other car. While I was deliberating on how I, supposedly the wise adult, should respond, one girl gently reminded the others, "My mom always says, 'If you can't say something nice, don't say anything at all.'" I expected an uncomfortable silence to follow, but it didn't. She laughed. "I think that's a pretty good idea, don't you?" The other girls said, "Yeah!" "My mom says that too!" One girl even said, "Thanks for reminding us, Becky." It was as simple as that.

In leading, I have tried to operate on the assumption that if people aren't doing what they are supposed to do, it is probably because they don't know what to do or how to do it. If we can accept that premise, it helps us be patient and refrain from criticizing. Then we can focus more on the person's strengths rather than on what we may perceive as his or her weaknesses. That leads us to concentrate on what we can do to help the person learn what to do and how to do it.

Listen and Communicate

When I was a counselor in a ward Young Women presidency, we planned with the Young Men presidency an event for the youth of the ward. The day before the event, we learned that the Young Women president was out of town and no one knew if she had completed her assignment. I don't even remember now what it was, but she was supposed to do something that was essential to having the event.

We tried every way we could to find out when she was coming back and if she had completed her task. Someone said they thought she was gone for a week. No one knew if she had done her assignment. For some reason, it must have been something nobody else could do. Also, we were young, inexperienced, and impetuous. The other counselor and I told the bishopric we thought we had no choice but to cancel the event, which we did. The next day—the day of the event—the president came home expecting everything to still be on schedule. She had made the arrangements, and we had fouled everything up. Was I embarrassed!

We didn't have enough information to have taken the action we did. Part of that was her fault for not communicating with us, but I accept responsibility for having been unwise. In addition, we took authority for making a change that was not really ours to make.

Since that time, I have tried not to make decisions or take action too impetuously. I know that even just a little time and investigation may reveal more information that could alter the direction I might take.

Our decisions are only as good as our information. In our Church callings, we need to gather and give information. We do this through listening and communicating information in various ways. The most effective leaders I have known are those who listen to their associates' observations, opinions, and ideas and consider carefully how these might impact decisions to be made and action to be taken.

There is a worthy precedent set for this process that I was privileged to observe while serving at Church headquarters. The leaders of councils and committees in which the General Authorities serve try to utilize the experience and wisdom of the Brethren who are members of those councils. I have observed the Brethren giving detailed reports on research they have done on a given matter that was under consideration at the time. The others listened intently, asking questions to clarify understanding.

Each time our presidency went before the Priesthood Executive Council to give a report on Primary or to make a proposal for a course of action regarding the children of the Church, we found a receptive audience in the members of the council. They listened attentively. Their attention, questions, and aside comments and conversations communicated to us that they sincerely wanted to hear and consider what we had to report or propose. Even when outcomes were not what we had hoped for—and that sometimes happened—we were satisfied that our position had been heard and carefully considered. As a leader, you need to listen. Listening is vital.

And so is communicating.

It is important for everyone to have the opportunity to communicate their ideas and observations, or those ideas and observations will not have the chance to be heard. As a leader, you need to let your associates know that you expect their input, and then give them an arena in which to present their contributions.

Some auxiliary leaders meet regularly with each of their board members to listen to their candid observations about their responsibilities, and to invite them to make suggestions. This adds to the leader's store of information and gives board members opportunities to think creatively about how to improve the effectiveness of the group.

When our board members made a report on the status or progress of a committee, they used a format we had given them. We asked that they report the name of the committee, the purpose of the committee, committee members' names, what they were currently working on, a summary of any information they might have gathered, conclusions they had reached, and recommendations they might have. When you give people a format to guide them, you are communicating your expectations as well as giving them an opportunity to communicate with you. This helps people focus their efforts while proceeding according to their inclinations and inspiration.

Such a process is based on sincere respect and true regard for others. It fosters unity rather than frustration and discord, because all viewpoints and perspectives are presented. Each person involved has the satisfaction of knowing that they have been part of the decision-making process, and usually they can better accept the decisions made, regardless of the direction the final decision takes.

Keep Pride in Check

Leaders who are able to accept others and who listen and communicate best are those who are able to shut pride out of the process, or at least keep it in check (can any of us totally eliminate pride?). It is too easy to think your ideas or ways of doing things are the only and best ways. One talented leader said, "There usually are many ways to do things right." I have come to know that this is true, as long as we are doing the right things. Of course, there aren't many ways to perform specific ordinances or to make specific covenants. But in leadership styles and practices, it just may be that someone else has a better idea than yours. Be open to that possibility.

When I start getting emotional about a situation, it helps me to ask myself occasionally, "Is pride a factor in this? Are my feelings based on pride?" Usually the answer is yes. Pride makes us say things about others and do things we are sorry for later. Recognizing pride as a possible source of these feelings that cause disunity can often be enough to eliminate the prideful feelings. Sometimes it is necessary to pray for a reduction of pride so we can see circumstances and conditions as they really are.

If we can keep pride in check, we can make great strides in accepting others, listening to and communicating with them, and blessing their lives. With unity we will have a greater capacity to move toward our goals.

Involve Others Meaningfully

Church research has shown that one of the deciding factors in conversion and retention of members is the meaningful involvement of members in Church activity and service. Meaningful involvement helps the member make an active contribution to the Church and helps the gospel become his or her way of life. Involving others meaningfully generates unity within an auxiliary, class, or committee.

A friend of mine wrote, "As a new stake Relief Society presidency and board, we decided that we would do everything for our first stake women's conference. We wanted the sisters to be able to just come and enjoy without all of the work and worry. To our disappointment, the attendance was lower than we had anticipated. When we evaluated the conference, we decided that we had made a poor decision to do it all ourselves. We realized that people like to be involved and that they have wonderful ideas and talents. For all our other functions, we involved as many sisters as possible, and all were well attended. We learned a good lesson that I now apply in all my callings."

Each member needs important work to do. Everyone needs to be able to see their work as affecting the lives of others in positive ways, as Moses did during his instruction by the Lord. When the Lord showed Moses the history of the earth, including the ministry of the Savior and the end of the world, Moses could understand that his calling involved far more than just leading a group of people from one land to another. He was to help prepare a people to receive Jesus Christ, who would redeem the world. (See Moses 1:27–39.)

Leaders today also need to help their associates understand the eternal nature of the service they are giving. Leaders can do this by bearing testimony, reading pertinent scriptures with their associates, praying together, calling attention to the results of their associates' service, and being an example of faith and commitment.

The relationships that form in a united presidency can be deep and abiding. A former Relief Society president wrote, "Our presidency and secretary were totally united. We were as close as sisters. At our meetings, the atmosphere was such that everyone made suggestions and we prayed and considered and discussed all ideas before making a final decision.

"After a special stake meeting where cancer in women was discussed, we joked a little about the fact that one in four women contract cancer, and we wondered which of our four it would be. Two years after that meeting, one of the counselors, Peggy, died of cancer. I have a cross-stitch she gave me that says 'Forever Friends,' which I treasure, because I know we will be friends forever."

Unity is not a finish line to cross and then dismiss as no longer relevant. Striving for unity is an ongoing process that needs constant nourishing. Don't be discouraged if you don't seem to be getting there, because unity develops slowly. If you continue to accept others, avoid criticizing others, listen and communicate, keep pride in check, and involve others meaningfully, you can continue building unity among the members of your group.

CHAPTER SEVEN

Working Effectively with Priesthood Leaders

Wherefore, he that preacheth and he that receiveth,
understand one another, and both are edified
and rejoice together.
—D&C 50:22

What do you think are the major challenges in implementing the purpose and program of your auxiliary? If you asked your bishopric, high council, or stake presidency adviser that question, what would he be likely to answer? Would his response be the same as yours?

If you tried that exercise as an experiment, you may find that your list of challenges would be different from your adviser's list. When we asked the same question in training sessions, we found that usually the women would list such concerns as teachers' commitment and tenure, inadequate teaching space and supplies, children's behavior and attendance, and quality of teaching. Their bishopric adviser would often list such things as staffing problems, budget inadequacies, time constraints, and parents' lack of support.

The reason that the lists were seldom the same was not only that men and women are different in some ways, but also that their assignments and perspectives were different. Each perceives the challenges of leading an auxiliary according to past experience and what he or she sees each week, and they don't usually see the same things. So their information, perspectives, and attitudes are different.

It is interesting to note that the more alike the lists were, the more likely the women leaders and their bishopric were to be communicating effectively and working well together. From this I have concluded that *there is direct correlation between the children, young women, and adult women in a ward having a positive gospel experience in their organization, and the effectiveness of the working relationship of the women leaders and their bishopric.*

The most effective of these men and women leaders seem to be unified because, first, they know and carry out their respective duties as given in the handbooks. In addition, they return again and again to the handbook to learn how to be leaders and how priesthood and auxiliary leaders interface. They are able to accept differences, listen and communicate information, keep pride in check, see their work as meaningful, and refrain from criticism. Women who want to work effectively with men need to understand the principles of unity, as discussed in chapter 6. These form the foundation for working together harmoniously.

Much of what is written about gender differences, while often true, tends to overgeneralize. However, social scientists seem to agree that there are some inherent differences that affect how we interact with one another. This is directly related to our working together in the Church.

For example, men tend to be "bottom-liners." They want to get right to the point. Women, on the other hand, may lead up to a point by setting the stage with information. Because of our different experiences, we often have information men don't have. We also have some intuitive feelings that can be part of the information we convey.

Generally, a man would rather have a woman get to the point at the beginning of the conversation. He may become impatient while the woman is setting the stage because he wants to know what he needs to "fix." Sometimes he may even stop listening until she gets to the bottom line. If a woman feels intensely about a matter, she really wants something to happen. She feels that if he doesn't listen to all she has to say, he won't have the information he needs to understand in order to take effective action.

Instead of getting angry or frustrated with priesthood advisers, we can modify our need to express ourselves, and get to the point quickly. In a meeting with an adviser, be concise in your discussion about each item on the agenda. For example, if you are reporting an event, state briefly what took place at the activity or meeting, give an example of some positive results, then go to the next agenda item.

In matters of problem-solving you might try proceeding something like this:

—State briefly the problem or matter to be considered.
—Give pertinent information about the matter. (What do you think is the cause? What are the existing conditions?)
—Tell what solutions or courses of action you have considered.
—Suggest a proposed course of action.
—Ask your adviser's counsel. (Does he have additional information that you may not have considered?)
—Listen carefully to his counsel.

I have seen this procedure work very well with most advisers. However, some advisers may not let you get beyond stating the problem. They jump right in with their opinions and solutions. If your adviser tends to do this, be patient. You may be able to avoid this situation by telling him at the beginning that you have a problem to discuss—that you would like to give him some pertinent information and discuss some of the solutions you have considered. If he knows where you are going, and you go there quickly, he will be likely to listen.

Another communication problem women sometimes have with men is one I heard a speaker experienced in working with men describe at a BYU women's conference. She noted that in a discussion a man often likes to "spar" and considers it a compliment if another man deems his idea worthy of critiquing. A woman, on the other hand, tends to get defensive if her idea is not accepted without question. If a man starts tossing her idea around to consider its pros and cons, she tends to take it as a personal affront, when he is probably just considering all the options and may even assume that his attention to the matter is a compliment.

When I recognized this aspect of men/women communication, I relaxed and started enjoying the idea-sharing process, rather than thinking my ideas weren't getting through. It rid me of a feeling I think was probably very closely related to pride, and which had caused me to feel defensive and combatant. It might work that way for you too.

If you are not having regular meetings with your adviser, ask for them. He may not even know he needs to meet with your presidency or committee. He may not know you need his help.

Make it easy for your adviser to help you. Some of the following suggestions might work for you:

Have a written agenda for each meeting with your adviser. You could offer to prepare it and give it to him in advance of the meeting. On the agendas for our meetings with our advisers, the first item was "Information from [adviser's name]." This way he knew what to expect and could prepare by thinking about actions taken or information received that might be helpful to us.

Follow up telephone calls or conversations with a written note to confirm decisions that were made. One leader I know gave her adviser a yellow folder with the name of her organization on the cover. She would then write all her written communications on yellow paper, and he would know to put it in the yellow folder. This way the papers didn't get lost. If a yellow page turned up in his other things, he knew what to do with it. And the yellow folder was easy to find when he needed something from it.

Make appointments with your adviser. Avoid camping outside the bishop's office or on his doorstep hoping to catch him in passing. Make an appointment, even if the meeting needs to be brief. He'll appreciate your organized approach and your consideration of his limited time. And he'll be better prepared to listen.

Ask for his counsel only on the most important matters. There is much that your presidency can solve on your own. Move ahead with what you can, and use your meetings with him for the big stuff. Then when you take a matter to him, he will know it's important and that he needs to be attentive. Be sure you have done your homework before the meeting.

Appreciate and acknowledge your adviser's help. I like men. They have taught me valuable lessons about life and about leading. Most advisers to auxiliaries sincerely want to do their best to help women leaders. If we assume and expect the best from them, we will probably get it.

When I was stake Primary president, we were fortunate to have a wonderful high council adviser who took his assignment with Primary seriously. He attended our executive meetings when we invited him, giving us valuable insights and wise counsel. He regularly conducted departments for bishoprics at our stake leadership meetings. He and our stake president were very responsive to us. We felt fortunate and blessed.

A stake Relief Society president wrote, "Brother Green quietly gave his constant support. We included him in everything. When we called board members to remind them of meetings, we called him too. He attended all monthly board meetings and Relief Society-sponsored events, sincerely offering his help. He would come the day or night before to help us prepare, doing those more difficult tasks that require a man's strength.

"He could have felt uncomfortable, because he was most

often the only man present. But because we treated him as an important part of the board—which he was—he felt accepted and free to offer his suggestions. We appreciated the strength that he contributed to our functions. He always sat on the stand and was introduced with our board. This wonderful man advised us for six-and-a-half years, and we admired and appreciated him."

Women in leadership positions in the Church need to appreciate their priesthood leaders and forgive them when they do not understand women very well. We mustn't fall into the trap of equating the human differences of our brothers and sisters with weakness in the Church or in the gospel. The gospel of Jesus Christ is true and perfect. We mortals in his church— all of us—are just learning how to live it.

I have seen much good accomplished because presidencies and their priesthood advisers were unified in the service they were giving. The General Authorities have frequently expressed their encouragement of such productive relationships. In a conference message Elder M. Russell Ballard said, "May God bless you, brothers and sisters, to find inspired consensus and unity as you counsel together in your service one to another. Only in so doing can the Church and our families begin to approach their full potential for doing good among the children of God on earth." ("Strength in Counsel," *Ensign,* November 1993, p.78.)

CHAPTER EIGHT

"For the Power Is in Them"

Verily I say, men should be anxiously engaged
in a good cause, and do many things of their own free will,
and bring to pass much righteousness; for the power is in them,
wherein they are agents unto themselves. And inasmuch as
men do good they shall in nowise lose their reward.
—D&C 58:27–28

When I was stake Primary president, I often wondered what the general Primary leaders talked about in their meetings. What concerned the presidency and board the most? How did they arrive at their decisions? I would have loved to know the inside scoop. Little did I know how much "inside" I would eventually get! The truth is, I learned many lessons while serving at Church headquarters, and one of the most important is the topic of this chapter. Through it your vision may be expanded, as mine was.

Let me begin with a story. Chelsea, age four, slipped her little feet into her Sunday shoes as her mother explained that Chelsea would be changing Primary classes that day. "But I like my class," Chelsea argued. "I want to stay with Sister Merrill and hold her hand."

"Honey, all the children are changing classes today." Chelsea's brow furrowed. Her mother added, "It's really all right. You'll be fine."

Chelsea looked doubtful. "Well, okay." Then her face brightened. "I know! I'll take Sister Merrill with me!"

Like Chelsea, most people seem to like the security of familiarity. In our Church callings we like doing things the way we've always done them. Changes in callings, in programs, in boundaries, and in bishoprics can be traumatic for some. Like Chelsea, adults also have the tendency to want people to "hold their hands" or tell them everything to do in their callings.

That brings me to the point of this chapter: Within the established structure of the Church, and while adhering to the principles of the gospel, we need to seek and respond to the inspiration that comes to us. We should not expect Church leaders to tell us every step to take. It would be contrary to the eternal principle of agency. "For behold, it is not meet that I should command in all things" (D&C 58:26).

Compulsion was whose plan? It was the gross lie of the originator of lies—that we could be compelled and still return glorified to our Father in Heaven. But therein is the lie—there is no glory, no reward in compulsion.

Throughout eternity we have been, we are, and we will be commanded in some things, but not compelled in anything. We can choose. If we were compelled in all things we would be robbed of our agency and of the opportunity to receive our own inspiration.

It is my feeling that when the Lord says we should "do many things of [our] own free will" (D&C 58:27), he expects us to use our agency and initiative to take action, to move our lives and his work ahead, and to do good.

Leadership in a Worldwide Church

It is neither possible nor wise for the Church to give us all the details we need to fulfill the responsibilities of our callings, because we are an international church. We have millions of members in many thousands of congregations all over the world. It won't be long before members worship in nearly two hundred languages. The gospel is indeed filling the earth. The Lord has directed the work of the Church in such a way that we have been organized and ready to accommodate world changes. The fall of the Berlin Wall and the dissolution of the Soviet Union, for example, have allowed the gospel to spread into previously inaccessible areas of the world. It is a glorious day in which we live. "His purposes fail not, neither are there any who can stay his hand" (D&C 76:3).

And you are part of that! Think of it! You are part of the timetable of the Lord. You have been allowed to participate in bringing to pass the "immortality and eternal life of man" (Moses 1:39).

Because of this rapid expansion, the demand on Church resources is enormous. The Church needs to provide what those millions of members around the world need most.

And what is that?

Brother Viacheslav Efimov and his wife, Galina, from St. Petersburg, Russia, helped me understand what members need. They had been members of the Church for about three years when they visited me in my office. Brother Efimov was then serving as a district president.

We listened intently as their young adult daughter translated her parents' description of the conditions of the Saints in their country—tiny groups of people meeting in humble homes or rented rooms. At that time they had no lesson books, handbooks, or hymnals. They knew just a few hymns the missionaries had taught them. Selected scriptures had been translated.

They described the poverty of their fellow Saints, who were grateful for shipments of clothing from Church Humanitarian

Services. Their faces reflected the radiance of their testimonies as they expressed their devotion to our Father in Heaven. Tears of happiness rolled down Sister Efimov's face as she told of her gratitude in knowing that the Lord loved them enough to allow them the hope and joy they had found in the gospel.

They were most concerned about their Primary children, recognizing that the future of the Church in their land lay with the children. The Efimovs had visited some Primaries in the United States and felt that their own simple Primaries were not adequate. We reminded them that they had what they needed for the blessing and benefit of the children—they had testimonies to share, scriptures to teach, and hearts that loved the children. We told them that sometimes less is more, because when we have less, we focus on what is most important.

It will be helpful when the Efimovs and their fellow Saints have more priesthood leaders, and when more scriptures, handbooks, and lessons are translated. But they have a basic Church organization to help unite them so they can teach, serve, and strengthen one another. They have opportunities to develop testimonies. And the time will come when they will have the blessings and covenants of the temple.

These things they cannot do without. You and I cannot do without them. They are basic, vital, unchanging needs, wherever we are.

Can you imagine the challenge of providing just these basic elements for millions of people worldwide in nearly two hundred languages? Church resources need to be used wisely in fulfilling these basic spiritual needs. Think about that the next time you wonder why we reuse our manuals and why handbooks aren't updated more frequently. It takes money and people to translate. We need to use these resources for what is most important.

In addition, the Church cannot complicate the programs so much that members anywhere lose sight of the mission of the Church and the most important principles and practices of the gospel of Jesus Christ. Our leaders have prioritized, and so must we.

In light of prioritizing, it seems to me that we need to think very carefully, for example, about planning Halloween parties, video game tournaments, sleepovers, or other entertainment for our members. We need to think about what gospel purpose these will achieve. I believe we should not do for our members what their families or the world can do for them, but we should do instead what the Church does best—teach the gospel. We can do it in interesting, enjoyable, even fun ways, but it should have a gospel purpose. That's being careful of our resources.

Being Spiritually Self-Reliant

Brother Jussi Kemppainen and his wife, Raijh, visited me in my office one day. This wonderful couple was from Finland. Brother Kemppainen was first counselor in the Finland East Mission. He was responsible for organizing branches of the Church in the Soviet and Baltic States.

They told me about the first time they visited a certain branch, where there were about thirty or forty people present. The Kemppainen family sang for the congregation "I Am a Child of God," a song these members hadn't heard before. When the Kemppainens returned seven weeks later to this little branch, there were approximately fifty people in attendance. Someone asked if their family would sing "I Am a Child of God" again. When they began to sing, much to the family's surprise and delight the congregation joined in singing. In that short time a musician living in the branch had translated the song into Russian and had taught it to the members. He saw what could be done to bless his branch, and he did it.

Beyond what the Church can properly provide, it is the sacred responsibility of local leaders and individuals everywhere to see what needs to be done and to do it. Collectively and as individuals, we can be more inspired, more efficient, and more effective in our methods as we fulfill our callings.

You are one of those leaders. You need to be open to the promptings of the Spirit to know how to help others find joy in the gospel. You can receive that guidance if you study your options and go to your knees. You can be inspired to know what the women in your ward need in a Sunday lesson. Activities you plan for young women can strengthen their testimonies. Your sharing times can be custom-designed for the children in your ward.

Proverbs 16:9 teaches, "A man's heart deviseth his way: but the Lord directeth his steps." I like the feeling I get from this verse, that of being a team with the Lord: I figure out the course I need to take, and if it is right he will strengthen me, inspire me, and guide me along the way.

The footnote to that scripture refers to the second chapter of Ether, in which we are reminded of the brother of Jared and how he and the Lord worked together to get light in the barges. The Lord asked the brother of Jared what he wished him to do. So the brother of Jared had to think it through and figure out what he needed the Lord to do.

You can be like the brother of Jared. You can figure out what you need, and inasmuch as you do good, you will receive the inspiration you need. The Lord is depending on you and expecting you to act.

That is not to say that you have the right to disregard the commandments, the teachings of the prophets, or the established Church organization. To do many things of your own free will does not mean you don't need the Lord or the Church. Agency is not criticizing the Lord's anointed servants. It is not disregarding instructions found in the handbook. It is not presuming to receive inspiration for people and programs that do not fall within your stewardship. It is not presuming to receive inspiration for people and programs *within* your stewardship that is contrary to direction from the Lord's anointed servants and Church policy.

It is my feeling that to do many things of our own free will means to utilize all the resources our Father has given us, including the scriptures, the words of the prophets, Church handbook guidelines, counsel from priesthood leaders, and our talents and training. Valid inspiration and revelation will harmonize with established Church procedures and revelations.

President Spencer W. Kimball wrote about what we can expect as we seek for inspiration in our lives and in our callings: "The one who receives revelation for any part of the Church, if his revelations are from God, will always be in the same direction as the general program the Lord has revealed to his prophets. In other words, the Lord will never reveal to a bishop a new program entirely contradictory to the program of the Church, even for his own ward. His revelations . . . will be more or less confirming and amplifying and giving further details." (*The Teachings of Spencer W. Kimball,* ed. Edward L. Kimball [Salt Lake City: Bookcraft, 1982], p. 453.)

So, as you exercise your agency and increase your own spiritual sensitivities, to ensure that the decisions you make regarding the direction of your life and Church responsibilities are in harmony with the gospel, you might ask yourself some questions that I learned from my friends who served with me on the Primary General Board.

One question might be, *"Is my decision or course of action in harmony with the scriptures?"* The teachings of the Lord are very clear in the scriptures. And the results of decisions made by people whose lives we read about in the scriptures are very obvious. When they followed the Lord, they were able to progress in many ways. When they disobeyed, disaster eventually followed.

The individual stories recorded in the scriptures are helpful to consider when we face similar situations. When Nephi broke his bow of fine steel, did he stand around complaining like the others did? No, he assessed his resources, used what he did have, sought and followed the counsel of his priesthood leader (his father) and the direction of the Lord, and was then successful in finding food. He took initiative and exercised his agency, all within the framework the Lord has established. (See 1 Nephi 16:18–32.)

How did Moses respond when Satan confronted him, lying

that he was the Only Begotten? Because Moses was intimately acquainted with the Lord, he knew Satan was an imposter. He was able to overcome Satan's lies because he knew the truth. (See Moses 1:12–22.)

A second question you might ask yourself is, *"Is my decision or course of action in harmony with the teachings of the prophets?"* Through natural processes of life and death, the Lord allows those of his servants whom he wishes to come to the head of the Church. President Kimball taught, "Since the death of his servants is in the power and control of the Lord, he permits to come to the first place only the one who is destined to take that leadership. Death and life become the controlling factors." ("'We Thank Thee, O God, for a Prophet,'" *Ensign,* January 1973, p. 34.)

It is through the Lord's prophets and those who serve under his direction that he directs his church. They hold the keys of authority to "preach the gospel and administer in the ordinances thereof" (Articles of Faith 1:5). "The Lord will never permit me or any other man who stands as President of this Church to lead you astray," taught President Wilford Woodruff. ". . . If I were to attempt that, the Lord would remove me out of my place, and so He will any other man who attempts to lead the children of men astray from the oracles of God and from their duty." (Doctrine and Covenants—Declaration 1.)

If we want to be in harmony with the Lord, we need to be in harmony with his prophets. If we make decisions that are in harmony with the teachings of living prophets, we can be assured that we are following what the Lord would have us do.

A third question to ask yourself is, *"Is my decision confirmed in my heart through prayer?"* I met a dear woman in Australia who demonstrated considerable dependence upon the confirmation of the Spirit. She had grown up in economically deprived circumstances and had not learned to read in her youth. When she and her husband joined the Church, she was called to teach Primary.

She spoke to us of her love for children—her own and the children in Primary—and how much she had enjoyed teaching them. We asked how she had been able to teach the children in Primary if she couldn't read the manual. Her reply continues to inspire me whenever I think of it. She said, "I knelt by the side of my bed with the lesson manual open on the bed. Then I prayed and prayed and prayed until Heavenly Father told me in my heart what I should teach the children."

This woman's experience illustrates that decisions and courses of action can be confirmed in our hearts through prayer. I have no doubt that the Lord put into her heart what he wanted the children to learn. She still didn't read very well when I met her and she was serving as the stake Primary president. I'm not sure she understood all of what was in the handbook. Nevertheless, she told me that her goal for the children of her stake was that they would feel the Spirit of the Lord when they came to Primary. She was dependent upon the Spirit to guide her, and that resulted in her doing what was most important.

You too can have your decisions and actions confirmed in your heart through prayer as you rise to meet your challenges and be what the Lord is expecting of you.

"For the power is in them, wherein they are agents unto themselves. And inasmuch as men do good they shall in nowise lose their reward." (D&C 5:28.) You can be anxiously engaged in your calling to lead. Your good cause can help many to live the gospel and find joy in doing so. The gospel can solve the problems of life and of the world. You can help bring that to pass in your life and in the lives of those around you.

CHAPTER NINE

Knowing What and Who Can Help You

My help cometh from the Lord.
—Psalm 121:2

Leading sometimes feels lonely. But you are not alone. When the Lord calls you to serve in any calling, he provides many opportunities for you to receive help.

Recognizing Heavenly Father's Help

Your most powerful—and always accessible—source of help is your Father in Heaven. He has blessed us with the Holy Ghost, who, in addition to other functions, enlightens our minds, helps us know what to do, and comforts us. When you humbly approach Heavenly Father in prayer, he can make his will known to you through the feelings you receive and the thoughts that come into your mind.

We were sitting together in an executive meeting of the Primary General Presidency when we received word of a decision by the Brethren that was not what we had hoped it would be. The information produced feelings of considerable anxiety in all of us. But as we were processing our feelings about the matter, a sudden wave of peace enveloped me. I felt a discernable difference between the anxiety of one moment and the peace of the next. In the midst of our conversation, I said quietly, "It will be all right. I know it will be all right." And in the next few months we saw decisions made that were even better than the one we originally had hoped for.

This experience reinforced for me the reality of the watchcare our Father in Heaven keeps over his children—even me! I needed that reassurance, and it came.

You can have that kind of help too. Mine was an unusually powerful feeling, but I have found that usually the feelings are more subtle. If you listen with your heart, you can know what to do.

Sometimes a high anxiety level restricts us from feeling the promptings of the Spirit. It is important not to force an answer. Try to be calm and patient. Trust the Lord, "wait upon" him (Isaiah 40:31), and recognize and act on the feelings you receive when they come to you. Sometimes help comes at unexpected times or in unexpected places, when you simply aren't thinking about your problems. My thoughts during the sacrament or during a Sunday School lesson or sacrament meeting talk often are the answers to what has been worrying me.

Try always to be worthy of the spiritual help you need. There are often times when I ask myself, *Is there something I need to be doing to make myself more receptive to the promptings I need to feel or hear? Are my prayers regular and specific? Do I need to attend the temple, fast, or be more diligent in my scripture study?* I learned those contemplative questions from a friend. She told me that she felt some of the success she and her husband had with their wayward son was a result of their asking themselves those questions. They had tried everything they could do to influence him and decided the only thing left was to perfect their own lives more. They felt that if they did this, at least they would have more chance of having him in eternity, even if he didn't repent in this life.

How the Ward Family Can Help

Often the Lord's help comes through another person. Regardless of your own family situation or the particular calling you have right now, you belong to a ward family. The members of your ward family are a built-in source of help to you in your calling. Each member of the ward family is part of a network of support and help. You are part of that network. You help others and others help you.

Virginia H. Pearce, while serving as a counselor in the Young Women General Presidency, said that the ward is a "place where there is enough commitment and energy to form a sort of 'safety net' family for each of us when our families cannot or do not provide all of the teaching and growing experiences we need to return to Heavenly Father" ("Ward or Branch Families: Part of Heavenly Father's Plan for Us," *Ensign,* November 1993, p. 79).

If you are a president, you have counselors, other leaders, and probably teachers to help you. In addition, you have a member of the bishopric with whom to counsel. No matter what your calling is, there is someone to help you. That is one reason we have a ward or stake organization—so no one has to be alone in a calling. If you don't know who those people are, ask. Someone will know.

Other valuable sources of help to a president are the presidents of the other auxiliaries. The general presidencies of Primary, Young Women, and Relief Society currently are housed in the same building, with their administrative offices on the same floor. They are able to meet together to discuss how they can unitedly strengthen children, young women, and adult women, and many good things have been achieved because of these meetings.

Stake and ward leaders often find that when they understand the needs of the others, they too are better able to understand how to strengthen the members for whom they have responsibility. Talking together from time to time can help achieve this understanding.

Discussions could include such topics as facilitating the transition of twelve-year-old girls into the Young Women program and young women into Relief Society, strengthening families, fostering unity among those serving in all three organizations, and sharing ideas on meeting the challenges of the individual organizations. When all are committed to unity and equity among them, this kind of collaboration has been fruitful.

Sometimes it may appear that people in the ward family are unwilling to help you. It is my feeling that this usually is because they don't know what is needed, what to do, or how to do it. Ask questions. Make suggestions. Don't hesitate to help others know how they might assist you in your calling.

Help from Church Publications

A vital and often overlooked source of help is information found in Church-produced handbooks, manuals, bulletins, and letters from General Authorities. These represent the official policies and approved procedures of the Church. You can be assured that you are conducting your particular Church assignment appropriately when you do so according to the information and instructions contained in these publications.

I learned this for the first time from a counselor in our presidency when I was stake Primary president. She had served with my predecessor, and she told me at our first presidency meeting how much she had appreciated the care with which the former president had studied and followed the instructions in the handbook. I learned to turn to the handbook each time I had a question. Usually the question was answered directly in the handbook. I learned that if the answer wasn't in the handbook, we were to study it out and receive our own inspiration and direction.

My experience at Church headquarters taught me further just how vital the instructions from Church headquarters are. Part of that understanding came when I learned how precisely the handbooks and other instructional materials are produced. The process is not a capricious one. Preparation is deliberate and includes several levels of review, not only by diligent and inspired Church service writers and professional staff but also by general officers (auxiliary presidencies and boards) when applicable, by General Authorities, and by the First Presidency.

The process takes time—sometimes years—in order to ensure doctrinal correctness and general correlation with Church programs, and to have a publication that is as refined and of as high a quality as possible. This is not to say that mistakes aren't made. But we can be confident when using Church publications that they are as inspired and accurate as it is possible to make them.

Because I know this, I would be hesitant to act or teach in a way that was not harmonious with the contents of Church handbooks, manuals, bulletins, and letters from the General Authorities. This does not mean that we can do only what is written in official documents. We need to be able to act for ourselves, but within the guidelines set by the Lord.

I like an illustration of this point that I heard described by an outstanding Church leader. He talked about my husband, Leonard, who is a landscape architect and planner. Leonard's business includes developing designs for the use of various kinds of properties. After the designs are complete, his firm prepares detailed drawings and specifications for how the projects are to be built. For example, the specifications could include such details as the type and quality of pipes to be used for an irrigation system. Contractors submit bids for the privilege of constructing the project. When a contractor is awarded a project, he is obligated to follow the drawings and specifications. He is at liberty to use equipment, personnel, techniques, and methods he likes best, but he must produce the results specified in the drawings and specifications. If he uses a sprinkler pipe of lesser quality than was specified, and the pipe breaks and damages the property, then he is responsible for the damage.

I feel that handbooks and other Church materials serve that purpose for us. They are safeguards. We do have a great deal of latitude within the guidelines—remember, we are counseled to act for ourselves to bring to pass much good. But if we function outside the guidelines, we are responsible for the results, whatever they may be. Further, I have seen those who expend much energy searching for "outside" materials or trying to find ways to sidestep or disregard guidelines, when it would have been easier, quicker, more accurate, and more productive simply to follow the handbook.

I believe following established, approved procedures and policies found in the handbooks is a way of demonstrating our willingness to be obedient to the Lord. Such obedience entitles us to his inspiration.

Now, having said that, I must point out that you will surely encounter others who do not feel this way. It will help you to remember that you cannot impose obedience on others. You can, however, inform and teach correct principles so that the choices made by others are at least informed choices. Good leaders who model themselves after the Savior teach correct principles with certitude and gentleness, inviting the Spirit to work upon and move those whom they are leading.

How the Scriptures Can Help You

The scriptures are a valuable resource to leaders. I learned this from Primary General Board members who led us in scripture study in board meetings. What we learned included problem-solving (see 1 Nephi 16:18–32), maintaining hope (see Ether 12:4–9), leading with charity (see 2 Nephi 33), and much more.

I also find that ideas and answers often come to me while I am studying the scriptures. Not that the answers are always there in so many words. I have never picked up the scriptures and had them fall open to a verse that seems to scintillate with the answer to the very matter that I have been pondering. It just hasn't happened that way for me. But a thought or impression will come to me as I am reading that gives me information, an answer, new hope, or peace. It may happen like that for you too.

How Statistics and Record-Keeping Can Help You

Statistical data is another source of help to leaders. Data is a means by which you can measure progress, and it is vital in making decisions. Statistics can help you know where you have been and where you are now. Then you can know where to go. For example, when you know which women did not have visiting teachers visit them last month, you can plan how to motivate their visiting teachers. When you know which young women are approaching age eighteen, you can plan how to contact them and encourage them to attend Relief Society.

Having statistical data at your fingertips also gives you support for your observations and suggestions when you are meeting and planning with other leaders. I learned that when I was a counselor to Primary general president Dwan J. Young. Once she called attention in the Priesthood Executive Council to the number of unbaptized nine-year-olds in the Church. By doing so, she generated attention to the situation and immediate action was taken. You too can call attention to potential trouble spots and help prevent problems from materializing by using statistics in meaningful ways.

Statistical information is relatively easy to obtain in the Church today. Your ward clerk has a wealth of computerized data that can be accessed quite easily. He is part of the ward family network that can help you, if you just ask. Your organization secretary can help too in collecting and analyzing data and assisting you to map trends that are occurring.

If we learn to recognize the inspiration the Lord is waiting to bless us with, and if we utilize the help of the ward family, Church publications, the scriptures, and statistical data, we will be assured that we have the very best help we could have.

CHAPTER TEN

Ideas for Problem-Solving

*You must study it out in your mind; then you must
ask me if it be right, and if it is right I will cause
that your bosom shall burn within you; therefore,
you shall feel that it is right.*
—D&C 9:8

"I don't want to do this anymore," the homemaking leader wailed. "I try to plan what will be interesting to everyone, but someone always complains!"

She had a problem. Lucky lady. How boring life would be if there weren't events or circumstances to challenge her thinking, stimulate her creativity, and build her character! Rather than approaching a problem as a negative drag on our progress, we can think of it as a gateway to greater accomplishment and satisfaction.

Problems can be solved. We don't need to throw up our hands and submit to apathy or despair. Doing that may actually be harder than identifying what needs improving and then attacking and solving it. We came to earth to solve the long thread of life's problems, and we can achieve that purpose. As leaders, we can be problem-solvers.

Nephi was a problem-solver. He had to be. He and his family had challenges that ranged from mere stumbling blocks to monstrous mountains. If he had not approached them as responsibly as he did, his family would never have reached the land the Lord had waiting for them. He was truly a leader.

Nephi identified problems, concentrated on one at a time, talked problems through with others, drew on all his resources, prayed, put his ideas into action, and gave thanks for the Lord's help when he succeeded. This is a process we could use as well. Consider how he dealt with the problem of his broken bow (see 1 Nephi 16:18–32).

Identify the Problem

Apparently Nephi was the only member of the family with a bow of fine steel. He and his bow must have been the main means for finding food, because he said, "And after I did break my bow, behold, my brethren were angry with me because of the loss of my bow, for we did obtain no food" (verse 18).

Problem identified: No food.

Some problems, like this one of Nephi's, are readily apparent. The lack of food was certainly such an immediate need to Nephi and his family that it was easy for them to identify their problem.

Sometimes we recognize problems only when we are constantly trying to find better ways to do things. This evaluating process is characteristic of good leaders. It is often while we are evaluating that we discover problems. As a leader you will be able to see some problems yourself, but when everyone is involved in identifying a problem, you are more likely to have a team of helpers to solve it. And you will be helping the others to develop their leadership skills as well.

Concentrate on One Problem at a Time

The urgency of the need of Nephi's family probably dwarfed any other discomfort they may have been experiencing, and it undoubtedly commanded Nephi's full attention.

Sometimes we become stimuli-bound in our Church responsibilities. Let's say you're part of a newly called Young Women presidency. Girls camp is two weeks away and there's no camp director, the Laurel adviser just had a baby and there's no one to teach on Sunday, yesterday the bishop wanted your plans for youth conference, and your two-year-old is sick.

Sound familiar? We often see many problems all at once and are immobilized by the magnitude of them. Instead, you might try making a list of everything needing your attention. Number the items in order of importance and focus on one at a time, starting with the most urgent or the one that, by solving it, will most help you accomplish what you want to have happen. The two-year-old needs to go to the doctor first. Then you can find a teacher for Sunday and go from there. Nephi had to attack the food problem before he saw to a broken tent or to Laman and Lemuel's latest quarrel.

Solve the most critical one. Then you can go on to others, one at a time.

Talk Through the Problem Together

Nephi wasn't blessed to have counselors, but he had a priesthood leader—his father. So he inquired of his father: "Whither shall I go to obtain food?" (Verse 23.)

When you discuss problems with your coworkers, you are helping them to invest themselves in the solving process, and you will often discover together many possible directions to take. Not all problems need to be discussed by everyone, but a presidency needs to talk together about most matters.

"Study it out in your [minds]" together (D&C 9:8). You could list and discuss all possible solutions suggested by the group. Then concentrate on those that you feel would bring the best results.

Some problems need the help of your priesthood adviser, as Nephi's did. It is interesting to consider that he went to his father—his priesthood leader—for counsel, even though his father had murmured. Nephi respected Lehi's position as the spiritual leader of the family and gave Lehi the opportunity to humble himself and receive strength as well as guidance.

Draw on All Your Resources

While Nephi didn't have steel from which to make a new bow, he did have access to wood, leather, and rocks, and he "did make out of wood a bow, and out of a straight stick, an arrow; wherefore, I did arm myself with a bow and an arrow, with a sling and with stones" (1 Nephi 16:23). Like Nephi, you can use what you have. For example, have you checked what the handbook says about the topic of your problem? That should be your first step. Many problems arise because leaders are not familiar with programs, procedures, or policies. Discuss together the resources available. This will help you find possible solutions.

Pray About the Problem, and Fast if Necessary

When Nephi asked his father for direction, Lehi prayed to know where to go to find food. "The voice of the Lord came unto my father. . . . And it came to pass that the voice of the Lord said unto him: Look upon the ball, and behold the things which are written." (Verses 25, 26.) Trust that Heavenly Father will help you solve the problem. He knows the answers and wants to help. He will help you feel when it is right (see D&C 9:8).

Put Your Idea into Action Immediately

Nephi "did go forth up into the top of the mountain, according to the directions which were given upon the ball. And it came to pass that I did slay wild beasts, insomuch that I did obtain food for our families." (Verses 30–31.) Nephi was fortunate that his solution was immediate. That is often the case when we follow inspiration.

Sometimes, however, we don't realize the results immediately. The entire solution may not be clear at first. Nephi talked it over, used his resources, and inquired of his leader before he actually went to find food. The second step often becomes apparent only after you take the first step.

But if your first plan doesn't work, don't give up. Try another until your problem is solved. Keep in mind that it is not possible to please everyone. That was one thing bothering the homemaking leader described at the beginning of the chapter. Pleasing Heavenly Father *is* possible, and solving problems based on fundamental truths of the gospel helps ensure that your decisions are right and that he is pleased.

Rejoice and Give Thanks

When Nephi returned with food, "how great was their joy! And it came to pass that they did humble themselves before the Lord, and did give thanks unto him." (Verse 32.) Celebrate your successes! When the "Focus on Children" guidelines and suggestions were approved, our presidency took our supply of bubble solution out on the lawn south of our offices and blew bubbles to our hearts' content!

When we unitedly thank our Father in Heaven for helping us succeed, everyone recognizes that a problem has been solved, and we are less likely to care about receiving credit for ourselves. The scriptures do not indicate that anyone patted Nephi on the back when he returned with food, but recognition for contributions to success is important in helping people sense the importance of their work. As a leader, it is better if you don't expect credit, but it is good if you can see that other people are acknowledged for their roles in successful out-comes.

A friend once told me that she disliked using the word *problem* and avoided doing so as much as she could. She pre-ferred to use *opportunity for growth*. I like that and think of it often. I believe it is true. When leaders approach problem solv-ing in a methodical way, as Nephi apparently did, they find that problems have indeed become opportunities for growth.

CHAPTER ELEVEN

Making Time
Your Servant

To every thing there is a season,
and a time to every purpose under the heaven.
—Ecclesiastes 3:1

You own your time.

If you want to, you can manage much of that time to your own advantage. You can make time work for you instead of against you, so that at the end of a day, a project, or a calling, you can feel that you have done your best.

Clearly, total control of all our time is not possible in this life. Those who struggle for total control reap only frustration and discouragement, because it just doesn't happen. There is much of what happens in life that is not and should not be under our command, and we can make ourselves miserable trying to change this. It is a great relief to realize that working harder or smarter does not necessarily mean we will master all our time.

What we should hope for is to be able to manage our time in ways that bring enough order to our lives that we can move toward our goals without feeling that success is always just out of our reach.

I have identified four aspects of managing time that can help us do that:

—Getting organized
—Planning ahead
—Delegating
—Doing it

This summer I planned a family reunion. I tried to follow the steps listed above. One of my brothers commented at the reunion that he was impressed by how easy it seemed for me. Of course, he didn't see everything that had gone into it, but when the day came, it *was* easy. Well, maybe it wasn't exactly easy, but because I got organized, planned ahead, delegated, and then did it—processes that work for me—the reunion went just about as planned, and I didn't get anxious during the day.

This chapter is about how and why these aspects of time management work for me.

Getting Organized

Because I am not naturally organized, I have to work hard at this. But I've tried long enough that I've learned what being organized can do for me. I feel more in control, I can make things happen rather than let things happen, I can find things when I need them, and I can sleep better! Those results are worth my efforts.

Let's face it. What we do today is life. Real life. It's not out there somewhere in the foggy future, but right here and now. The reason we want to be organized is to make the here-and-now satisfying, and to make the present moment a step toward getting us where we want to be.

All things in the Lord's kingdom are done in order and in due time. Today the Church is organized under the order of the priesthood. The earth is being flooded with the gospel because the Church is organized in such a way as to facilitate missionary work, translation of scriptures, and transmission of prophetic messages. Even when a prophet dies there is no turmoil, no campaigning for position, no disarray. The orderly processes of priesthood leadership and succession function smoothly and precisely. Order is a pattern for us to follow so that we can thrive as individuals, just as the Lord's earthly kingdom has thrived.

"Organize yourselves; prepare every needful thing; and establish a house, even a house of prayer, a house of fasting, a house of faith, a house of learning, a house of glory, a house of order, a house of God" (D&C 88:119). As I contemplate this passage of scripture I see two things that are meaningful to me. One is that I need to organize myself. The second is that some things are needful, maybe more important than others. Both of these ideas are important to consider.

What things are the most needful?

The above scripture, referring to the temple that would be built, lists what is necessary for our happiness and our ability to progress: prayer, fasting, faith, learning, glory, order, a house of God. *Needful.*

There is a multitude of popular systems and methods of organizing—planners, seminars, books, even computer systems—based on this premise: spend your time doing what is most important to you. *Needful.*

When the Lord visited Mary and Martha, Martha prepared the meal while Mary listened to Jesus. When Martha complained that she was doing all the work, Jesus pointed out that "one thing is needful" and indicated that Mary had chosen to take advantage of a rare opportunity to learn of things eternal. (See Luke 10:38–42.) (We don't know everything about this incident, but I believe that what Martha was doing—preparing the meal—was also needful. I doubt that the Savior's words were intended to chastise her.)

The gospel helps us understand where we should focus as we plan and organize our lives. Jesus taught in the Sermon on the Mount, "Seek ye *first* the kingdom of God," and indicated that somehow we'd be able to get the other things done (Matthew 6:33; emphasis added). I know that to be true.

When you think about it, the whole purpose of the gospel is to make today satisfying and to get us to where we want to be. The prophets, the scriptures, the commandments, the Church organization, and the ordinances and covenants are given to help us accomplish this. They are to bring us peace and hope in this life and the eternal blessings our Heavenly Father has waiting for us in the life to come.

Here are some ideas for getting organized:

1. Have a place to work. At different times in my life my place to work has been my bed, the kitchen table, a desk, a corner of a room, and an office. With the advent of the computer age, more and more homes have a workstation, even if there is not a whole room available.

2. Have a place to put things. One day when I was about ten years old, my Grandmother Packer repeated a saying that I didn't understand until later. It was "A place for everything and everything in its place."

Gradually I came to understand that to have order, everything needs a place to be kept, and then it needs to be kept in that place when it is not being used. If there is not a place for something, make a place for it, or else give it away or throw it away. When I have had a mess around me, I often have repeated aloud what Grandmother said. When I have remembered this counsel, refreshed in my memory by prominent author and lecturer Daryl Hoole, the organization mentor of thousands of Latter-day Saint women of my time, I have been able to figure out a way to get rid of clutter and to streamline my life.

My husband will laugh when he reads this because—and I admit it—I have trouble keeping things in their proper places. I'm forever looking for my car keys, glasses, and shoes, for example. And I'm a messy cook. I don't clean up until I'm finished. When Leonard is in the kitchen with me, he wipes up the counter and puts things away. He's very helpful, even when he sometimes dispenses with ingredients or cooking utensils before I'm finished with them!

When I do keep things in their places, I find I can enjoy cooking, working, sewing, painting, or writing more because I know where things are and I don't waste time rifling through lots of stuff. For organizing paperwork, I started with a cardboard accordian-style file. It worked for me for several years. Gradually we added a desk, a bookcase to store Church manuals and reference books, and a small filing cabinet for such things as talks and articles I wanted to keep. Today, computers have the filing capacity that can reduce the need for cabinets.

Whenever you begin work on a lesson, meeting, or other assignment, if you are in your workplace and have everything in its place around you, you are organized to begin.

3. Use a notebook, calendar, or planner. When I was about to be released as Primary general president, I laughed with our board about having a ceremonial burning of my planner. But I didn't burn it. I just got a smaller one.

Despite all the jokes that are floating around about planners, you really need something to write your appointments, notes, and plans in. Bits of paper get lost, but with a notebook of some kind you can have everything available to you anytime you need it.

Years ago I had a small looseleaf binder with tabbed pages in it, even before planners were popular. Lots of folks did. A Relief Society counselor told me she still uses hers. She says she wants to tell *it* how to plan, not have a system tell *her* how. Whatever system you use, notebooks, calendars, and planners help you have a little more control of your time.

4. Make lists. List what needs to be done or remembered, and number each item according to its importance. Remember what is most needful to you and prioritize the most needful items first. Work on the list one item at a time.

A distant cousin of mine, a highly creative and productive woman, may spend a day, a week, or many months on one project. She says, "I just get everything together and then I work like crazy!" Women with families don't often have the luxury of uninterrupted time to stick with a project until it's finished. But even with interruptions, you can focus on your Relief Society lesson and complete your preparations before moving on to something else.

One of my friends makes her list for the next day just as she goes to bed at night. Others like to do it first thing in the morning before the family wakes up.

I often would have a daughter make a menu and grocery list while we were driving to a gymnastics lesson, to the mall, or to a piano lesson. We talked about what we wanted to have for meals that week, and she wrote it while I drove. That accomplished two purposes: We got the menus and shopping list done, and it also taught her a process she could (and does!) use in the future.

But I know a woman who doesn't make lists. She says it's a waste of time for her. Actually, she makes them in her head as she does other things. When she's driving, she plans what she's going to do first when she gets home. When she's on the phone, she's looking at a pattern guide for the dress she's going to make for her daughter. She'll know just what to do before she gets started. When she's folding laundry, she's planning her family home evening lesson. She says this is the kind of organizing that cuts time for her.

5. *Enjoy the process.* When work is necessary, it is valid, and we need to savor the feeling of using muscle, brain, and senses to perform the life support we do every day. I like the brain stimulation of organizing. I sense satisfaction as I check items off a list—I have even put things that I've already done on a list, just to be able to check them off! I relish how my back and arms feel when I'm stretching to reach things. I enjoy the smell of laundry detergent and fabric softener. The bite of crisp winter air stimulates my skin as I retrieve the garbage cans from the street. Even the cry of a baby is a beautiful sound. (Easy for me to say when my babies are grown and my sleep isn't interrupted, right?)

When we are doing what needs to be done, then what we are doing is worth something. And doing it well means a lot to the people we are doing it for. That makes rather holy the routine maintenance processes we go through every day. We need to savor it all.

Organization, then, can be an end in itself. But it is more than that. It is a means to an end. That's why leaders need to be organized. It is a way to help you help others more effectively.

Plan Ahead

Planning is what helps you make things happen. Once I said to a particularly well-organized friend, "Don't you ever do something on the spur of the moment just for fun?" She responded that she had fun because she planned ahead to get the fun started. She makes things happen.

We can each find a way to plan that works for us. Let me summarize the process I like to use:

Decide what you want to have happen. I learned this from the Young Women General Presidency under the direction of President Ardeth G. Kapp. We used the idea when we planned our recent family reunion. For example, we asked ourselves not "What do we want to eat?" but "What do we want to have happen?"

We wanted to build family relationships and to make some memories for everyone, especially the children. We wanted to do more than just entertain them, and we wanted everyone to feel they had contributed to the success of the reunion.

We could have ordered the corn from a market that husks and steams it and delivers it hot and ready to eat. Instead we had family members husk and cook it at the reunion. Some of them hadn't seen that done before. They chatted and laughed as they worked together, ripping off the husks and picking away at the corn silk. We chuckled as the squeamish turned up their noses at an occasional worm.

We could have picked up ice cream at the supermarket, but instead we made homemade ice cream. Some of the children had neither eaten homemade ice cream before nor seen it made. With Great-Grandpa in charge, several children put ice in the buckets and asked why we added salt to the ice, what the dasher did, and how long it would take for the mixture to become ice cream. Even twenty-two-month-old Mitchell diligently helped pick up some rock salt that was spilled. I believe some of the children will never forget that experience with Great-Grandpa.

In auxiliary work it is important that your goals are consistent with the purpose of the organization. This is one good reason for being thoroughly familiar with the handbook, where the purpose and goals are stated.

Understand existing conditions. Before you know where you are going, you have to know where you are. Who are you planning for? What are their concerns? What worries them? What makes them happy? What is their background? What has been done before? How did it work? How could it be better?

In a family, committee, or presidency, each member needs to express fully his or her viewpoint, experience, and feelings on a given situation. This way all those involved can understand the conditions that exist concerning the matter under consideration. This also allows everyone the privilege of contributing. This helps them be committed to the project too. As a leader you need everyone to invest themselves in what you are doing.

Establish priorities. Decide what task is the most important to accomplish first, or what you need to spend most of your time doing. When you establish priorities together as a group, you are all working from the same understanding. This helps focus your collective energy and also helps prevent conflicts that could arise from misunderstandings.

Make a plan. Making a plan means deciding how to accomplish what you want to have happen. Give everyone a meaningful assignment. Make sure each person understands the expected outcome of his or her assignment. Have in your minds what will happen to let you know that your plan has succeeded.

What conditions will exist then? What will people be doing or feeling? Will the results be measurable or observable?

Carry out the plan. Give yourselves some time to carry out your plan. Anticipate in advance what could go wrong, and try to remove those stumbling blocks before someone trips over them. Many leaders spend a great deal of energy trying to go around the obstacles, when removing the obstacle would be the most efficient and effective.

Evaluate. When your meeting, event, or project is over, talk about what worked, what didn't work, and what you could do differently next time. There is often a better way to do things. When you discover these better ways, you are growing as individuals and as a group.

Keep trying. If one plan does not work—and that happens frequently—try another one. Remember that the Lord knows how to solve the problem; your part is to be receptive to his inspiration. Depending upon the situation, you may need to wait for time to pass before trying again. Most matters we consider in the Church are worthy of real effort and persistence, but you need to be prepared to recognize and accept with poise and grace those that need to be let go.

Delegating

Delegating is another pattern set by the Lord. An example is found in Moses 1. When the Lord called Moses, he was offering Moses an invitation to share in his work "to bring to pass the immortality and eternal life of man" (verse 39). He also instructed Moses to delegate, in turn, some of his work to others, or he would "surely wear away" (Exodus 18:18).

It is essential for leaders to share their work with others in order to maximize the effect of the work. Through delegating, a group of people can achieve more together than any one of them could achieve alone. And this gives people the chance to grow.

In delegating you might follow these steps:

—Give assignments
—Allow authority to act
—Give responsibility for results
—Expect accountability

Give assignments. It is sometimes hard for capable people to delegate, because they hesitate to impose on others. They would rather do it themselves than ask someone else. Or they want to be sure it is done right, and they assume they are the only ones who can do it! Assigning responsibilities to others, however, is a compliment and a sign of trust.

In giving an assignment, be sure you are clear in your description of what needs to be done and when it needs to be completed. Help the person understand any ground rules, such as policy or budget. Let her know what resources are available. Before proceeding, make certain the person has accepted and is committed to the assignment.

Allow authority to act. Let the person know she has authority to move ahead and complete the assignment; then, once you have given the assignment, don't do it yourself. Doing it yourself releases the other person from responsibility, and may confuse and offend her.

Give responsibility for results. Let the person accomplish the assignment in her own way. Your methods might be great, but hers might be just as suitable as yours. So don't worry too much about how she is going to do it. Your concern is that the agreed-upon results are achieved.

Expect accountability. Arrange for a time and place when the person will report the results of the assignment. This helps stimulate responsible performance of duties and will assure you that you can relax about that particular task until the report is given.

Doing It

The short phrase "Do it," made popular in the Church by President Spencer W. Kimball, represents action. We can spend all our time planning, making lists, meeting, and talking, and never really get the job done. It is true that the best decisions are made with complete information, and every effort should be made to utilize all information. And that does take time. Decisions should not be made or action should not be taken capriciously.

But a true leader knows when to move.

I learned that from Dwan J. Young when I served as counselor in the Primary General Presidency. I have always been a deliberator. But when I saw Dwan confidently and competently move forward at a pace that took my breath away, I was inspired and energized. She was not capricious, but she knew when to move. Some matters do not need as much deliberation as others. And some situations call for immediate action.

One major deterrent to action, of course, is procrastination. I love the little verse quoted in a general conference by Elder Marvin J. Ashton:

> Procrastination is a silly thing,
> It only brings me sorrow,
> But I can change at any time!
> I think I will—tomorrow!
> (In "'Shake Off the Chains
> with Which Ye Are Bound,'"
> *Ensign,* November 1986, p. 14.)

Some of us make more work for ourselves and let things weigh on our minds too long when we put off doing what needs to be done. I notice that about my visiting teaching. I love the young adult women I am assigned to visit, and I thoroughly enjoy meeting with them and sharing ideas. So why I procrastinate doing it until the end of the month, I do not know. The fact that others procrastinate is not a good excuse. Eliminating procrastination from our lives would help us take the action that is characteristic of a good leader. As a leader, you need to be willing to step ahead, to get away from the planner and to just—do it.

CHAPTER TWELVE

Helping Others Develop
Strength and Commitment

*When ye are assembled together ye shall instruct
and edify each other, that ye may know how
to act and direct my church.*
—D&C 43:8

Joe, a young Church member with no previous teaching experience, was called to teach a Primary class. The bishopric felt that the ten-year-old boys needed a masculine influence at church on Sunday, and they thought Joe's youth and energy would be a good match for the boys.

When Joe was called, the bishop's counselor told him the age of the boys he would be teaching and that the Primary presidency would be contacting him. A counselor in the Primary saw him in the meetinghouse hallway, gave him his lesson manual, and told him where the Primary room was located.

Joe came to Primary the next Sunday with no idea of what to expect. He knew nothing about ten-year-old boys or about teaching. He fully expected the seven boys to be fascinated with the lesson he had prepared, but they weren't. They punched each other in opening exercises and refused to sing during singing time. By the time they got to the classroom, they were fidgety and disrespectful of their new teacher and of their surroundings.

When Joe stood in front of the class with his manual in hand, trying to get their attention, they were tipping backward on their chairs to see how close they could come to falling backward without actually doing so. He did the best he could to give some semblence of a good lesson, but with little success. He really wanted to do what he was called to do, and he tried for three more weeks to make a go of it.

At the end of the month he felt no better—in fact, he felt worse and worse each time he tried to teach the class. He felt like a failure. Finally he'd had enough. After Primary, he handed the lesson manual back to a member of the Primary presidency and said, "I've had it! This just isn't for me." And that was that.

What went wrong? Nobody likes to stay where they feel like a failure. No wonder Joe wanted to quit. He could see no other solution, so he simply bailed out.

Most people want to do what they've been called to do in the Church. And they do it in the only way they know how. If they don't perform as their leaders think they should, it's because either they don't know what to do or they don't know how to do it. That was true in Joe's case.

The role of leadership is to fill in gaps of information and skill, and to help structure the environment and experiences that will generate success for members serving in Church callings. In other words, *leaders need to teach others what to do and how to do it.* Leaders can strengthen the testimonies of those whom they lead, instill confidence through successful experiences, and prepare them for further responsibilities in the Church.

What could the leaders of Joe's ward have done to help him know what he needed to do and how to do it? He needed orientation as well as ongoing help and support.

Orientation

Orienting others is how a leader begins teaching what to do and how to do it. Orientation is what we need to know first about a calling. It is the overview of the who, what, why, when, and how of the calling. It is what gives a person the sense of knowing what the others who are serving with him or her know. It helps the person feel like part of the team, so to speak, and to feel that what he or she has been called to do is significant work in the Lord's church. An effective orientation helps people *want* to learn and grow.

Joe could have felt successful as a teacher if he had been oriented. He could have started with a solid foundation of preparation that could have helped him be and feel successful. Teaching the class could then have been a satisfying experience for him.

Orientation needs to take place as soon as possible after a person is called to serve, in a place away from distractions where both the orienter and the orientee can concentrate. The orientation is most effective when it is short and well organized, with a written agenda.

In order to conduct an effective orientation, the leader herself needs a clear vision of the responsibilities of the member she is going to orient. The basic responsibilities of callings in the Church are found in Church handbooks. When a leader is thoroughly familiar with the handbook information, and teaches that information, she can be assured that she is teaching correct principles. The handbook needs to be the framework of the orientation.

There is often other help and information that needs to be included in an orientation in addition to that found in handbooks. How do you decide what the member needs to know? Think of the Golden Rule. A capable leader from Idaho told me, "It helps me to put myself in the position of the person I'm orienting. I ask myself, 'What would I need to know if I had just received this calling?'" That's a good question. What would you need to know? "Orient unto others what you would have them orient unto you."

Here are some ideas:

Assurance and Confidence

First of all, if you were new in the same calling, wouldn't you need assurance that your calling is inspired of the Lord? Wouldn't you want to know that the presidency was grateful for your willingness to serve? I would hope they would express that appreciation.

I may be new to the Church, or young, or just returning to Church activity. I may be anxious about my ability to fulfill my calling. I would need my leader to express confidence in me and assure me that she will help me learn what to do and how to do it. It would have helped Joe to receive that kind of assurance from the Primary presidency.

So, as you begin to orient your new board members or helpers, assure them of your confidence in them and express your appreciation that they have accepted their call from the Lord to serve.

Purpose and Goals

If you were newly called, wouldn't you want to know the purpose or goals of the auxiliary or group you are serving with? This is the foundation for what you will be doing. Knowing the purpose will help keep you doing what is most important. It will help you prioritize what you do. Teachers, board members, and committee members often don't have copies of handbooks where such purposes and goals are found. So in orienting, it is important to turn to the handbook and teach the purpose and/or goals of the organization.

Specific Duties

Handbooks include descriptions of the duties or responsibilities associated with callings in the Church. Discussing these responsibilities is a critical part of orienting. Together, read in the handbook about the responsibilities of your orientee, and discuss the information. Some presidencies like to give the person questions and have her look up the answers in the handbook. Not only will you be teaching the person what she needs to know, but you will be setting a pattern for her to use a handbook to find information she will need in the future. Teachers also may need overviews of their particular courses of study as well as what the presidency hopes the teacher can accomplish with the members of the class.

People

If you were newly called, you would want to know with whom you will be serving. If you are a teacher, you need a list of the members of your class, and maybe you'd like to know who the other teachers are. If you are on the activities committee or the Scout troop committee, you need to know who the other members are. It would also help you to have a written list of their names, addresses, and telephone numbers.

Meetings

A Church member with a new calling needs to know what meetings to attend and what will be expected of her in those meetings. Lack of this understanding is often the cause of much frustration on the parts of both members and leaders. Nobody wants to go to meetings that are a waste of time. Some members will attend meetings out of duty or loyalty, but nearly everyone will want to have an experience that will be of benefit in some way. Let the orientee know how the meetings will benefit her.

Jenny, home from college for the summer, was called to teach a Sunday School class. She had not taught before and had some doubts about her ability. A member of the Sunday School presidency gave her the lesson manual and said something like this: "We have a ward in-service meeting next

Tuesday. Our young teachers like you are so busy and they usually don't come. But if you want to join us, the meeting starts at seven o'clock." I wonder how the novice teacher felt about her new calling at that moment?

What if the member of the presidency had said something like this: "We are so delighted to have you teaching some of our great young people. We know you are new to teaching, but we know they'll love you. If you are prayerful and give the lesson as it's outlined in the manual, you can be successful. The ward teacher-development leader gives regular lessons about teaching, and those lessons will be a big help. We all talk about our experiences in our classes, and we help each other a lot. I think you'll feel more comfortable about teaching if you will come to these lessons."

Resources

Your orientee needs to know what help is available. How will you support her? Who else can help? For example, what about the resources in the meetinghouse library? Is there specialized training available through the ward or stake, such as organist or chorister training, or training for family history, or Scouting skills training? Is there something available on video? Somehow an assignment seems less overwhelming when we realize how much help is available.

Local Goals

Often local authorities have given specific information, direction, or goals for Church members in their area. Such goals may include activating members, increasing temple attendance, or fellowshipping new members. Sometimes a stake presidency or bishopric will want to emphasize increasing spirituality, making sacrament meetings more worshipful, or holding regular family home evening. Members in new callings deserve to have this information to help keep them in harmony with the overall focus of local leaders.

Testimony and Prayer

A newly called member of your particular "team" needs to hear of your own faith and testimony. You are her leader, and she needs you to express your convictions concerning the Lord's work and the important part you both play in helping that to be accomplished in your own little part of the Church. In orienting, it is appropriate to include a prayer for the Lord's blessings to guide you both in the service you are giving.

Ideas for Ongoing Help

Once a member is oriented and serving, she needs ongoing support and help. There are as many ways to do this as there are leaders in the Church who are tuned in to the Spirit for guidance. When the intent of your heart is to strengthen and help those you are leading, and when you know them well, you will be prompted to know what they need.

I have found that the ongoing help people seem to need most falls into one of three categories: actual physical assistance, expressions of appreciation, or spiritual strengthening.

Physical Help

A friend of mine who serves as a counselor in a ward Relief Society told me she once telephoned a teacher and asked what she could do to help her with the lesson. The teacher nearly went into shock. Although she was a mature woman, both in age and in Church service, no one had ever called her before to offer assistance with a lesson.

When I was a stake Primary president, one of the ward presidents, Joyce, was called to be a counselor in our presidency. When I visited that ward following Joyce's call, the Primary secretary, a rather shy and newly reactivated sister, said to me tearfully, "You have taken my best friend!" I sympathized with her, because I knew she was sincerely mourning.

But I also rejoiced inside because I sensed from what the secretary had said that my new counselor would be able to generate the same kinds of feelings in the other ward leaders she would teach.

I asked the secretary why she felt so close to Joyce. She replied that Joyce had helped her know what to do and had shown her how to do it, staying right with her until she could function on her own. Some people need more autonomy than that, but Joyce had sensed the help this woman needed, and gave it. Later, my initial feelings about how Joyce would serve as a counselor were validated as I saw her give sensitive help specifically tailored to the women she was leading.

An outstanding Primary president once told me, "Our teachers need to know of our concern and love for them. They need to know that we are there for them emotionally and physically. Every Sunday, every teacher needs to have some kind of positive interaction with a member of the presidency, just as we expect the teachers to have with the members of their classes. 'How did your class go?' 'How's the problem with Matthew?' 'Is that suggestion we made working?' 'Thank you for being there for the children.' Teachers thrive under that kind of support, just as children do."

Expressions of Appreciation

Each of us needs to feel appreciated. We can never show too much appreciation to others; most of us don't show nearly enough. After a talk I gave on this subject, an energetic and confident young woman spoke to me. She told me how she had spent the past two years as a Primary teacher. She was now in another calling, but I could tell from her demeanor that she probably had been a wonderful teacher. She said she had enjoyed the children and she had enjoyed what she had learned from the lessons, but—and this was fascinating to me, coming from such an outgoing, confident woman—she said, "Those two years were the loneliest two years of my life."

What happens inside someone who feels like that? They have to be very self-motivated and firm in the faith to continue on in the calling and in the Church. Leaders cannot do everything for the people with whom they are serving, but they can do some things, and one is giving adequate support and sincere appreciation.

Even President Spencer W. Kimball longed for expressions of appreciation. "I find myself hungering and thirsting for just a word of appreciation or of honest evaluation from my superiors and my peers. I want no praise; I want no flattery; I am seeking only to know if what I gave was acceptable." (*The Teachings of Spencer W. Kimball,* ed. Edward L. Kimball [Salt Lake City: Bookcraft, 1982], p. 489.)

Spiritual Strengthening

Probably the most effective way of strengthening another is through sharing our own faith and testimony. When members' faith and testimonies increase, their motivation and commitment increase proportionately. If we want to help people become more diligent in their callings, we need to help them grow spiritually. This allows for the agency of the individual. It also is more effective than nagging and reminding and arguing.

Remember that you can't make people be better. You teach them and they make themselves better.

Our presidency and board enjoyed sharing insights and perspectives from the scriptures. We taught one another, bore our testimonies, and attended the temple together. These were highlights that none of us will forget. It is significant that when we were released, board members requested that our reunions include going to the temple and scripture study. These had become the most valued of our many experiences together. They were part of what unified and strengthened us.

In a Sunday School Gospel Doctrine class, I had been asked to lead a discussion about Job and how his family and friends responded to his trials. I asked the class to describe some of the ways others had strengthened them in hard times. After several appropriate responses, one brother said, "The very most helpful thing to me has been when people I love, respect, and admire remain constant and strong in their testimonies regardless of difficulties. They give me hope and courage to stay firm in my faith through my hard times."

As you function with others in your calling as a leader, pray together. Bear your testimony often, and allow others to do so. Call upon your favorite scriptural passages when others need strengthening. You may need to do some personal scripture study in order to prepare yourself to help others increase their spirituality.

If you will invest in that preparation, you will reap a harvest of new insights into the scriptures and into the solutions of your personal challenges and Church responsibilities. You will sense what your coworkers need from you. As you share your favorite scriptures, your favorites will become some of their favorites, and theirs, yours. You will work together in greater harmony, and together you will be fortified through the Spirit of the Lord.

CHAPTER THIRTEEN

∽

Conducting Meetings

Conduct the meetings as [you] are led by the Holy Ghost,
according to the commandments and revelations of God.
—D&C 20:45

Many years ago, Elder Spencer W. Kimball ordained my husband, Leonard, as a high priest when he was called as a bishop's counselor. The most memorable phrase to both of us from that blessing was something like, "Conduct meetings without facetiousness." He actually used the word *facetiousness.* To us at that young time of our lives, the message seemed to be, "Don't tell jokes." But Leonard was not a joker, so we had to start thinking about Elder Kimball's counsel in another way.

We have come to understand that Elder Kimball probably meant that Church meetings, in which a leader is the Lord's representative, are worthy of dignified, poised behavior by leaders. That is not to imply stiffness, coldness, or even lack of humor. The leader of a meeting in the Church needs to be warm and kind, and even relaxed.

The conducting official of a meeting in the Church helps set the tone, mood, or spirit of the meeting. Prelude music, congregational singing, and the messages of the speakers, as well as the spirit that members bring with them, all impact the spirit of the meeting. But the leader who is conducting may have the greatest influence on the feelings people experience while they are there.

We have seen the warmth, kindness, and even humor exhibited by members of the First Presidency as they conduct general conference meetings. Theirs is a good example for the rest of us. These leaders conduct in an orderly and efficient manner, without wordiness or too much casualness. They are flexible enough to make a comment on what has just happened, but the interjection is usually short, and an occasional humorous comment does not detract from the spirit of the occasion.

As the leader of a meeting, you can invite the Spirit to be present as well as inspire confidence in your leadership. To some, achieving this comes quite naturally, but most of us need to think about it and plan for it. Here are some things you can do to help you accomplish this standard of conducting.

Pray to Have the Spirit with You

The suggestions that follow are some rather mechanical aspects of conducting that can significantly affect the mood you help create, but none of them has the refining influence that comes with the presence of the Holy Spirit. The Spirit helps you speak and act "according to the commandments and revelations of God" (D&C 20:45). The Spirit speaks to the hearts both of the conducting official and of the members in attendance, and it teaches beyond what is actually said and done (see D&C 50:21–22).

Be Yourself, but Be Your Best Self

You have been called to lead because of what you have to offer, as well as for what the calling can do to help you grow. So be yourself—your best self—because you are the one whom the Lord called. When you are your best self, you expand your capacity and increase your ability.

One of the ways you can be your best self while conducting is to be well prepared. Know exactly what needs to be said and done in the meeting, and be sure that all the details are taken care of.

It is good to have a standard in your mind. Perhaps there is a role model, someone you know who inspires you when you see him or her conduct. That is one of the ways we learn from one another. It reminds me of the old "as if" theory I heard about years ago: You act as if you were already the person you want to be, and by doing the things that person would do, you grow into the habits and behaviors that help you become your best self. That is quite motivating to me.

"As if" behavior needs to be tempered, however, by the realization that the best you have to offer as a leader is you. You need to be happy with who you are and not be constantly frustrated by comparing yourself or competing with someone else. I could easily have become intimidated or discouraged in the presence of some of the outstanding women with whom I have served. But my prevailing feeling was that the Lord knew my heart, and he was the one I was striving to please.

See to Physical Arrangements

The place your meeting is held needs to be pleasant and comfortable for those attending. If you can control the temperature, do so. Open or close windows, doors, or draperies. Rooms that are too hot make people sleepy. When people are too cold, they may not get sleepy, but they have a hard time concentrating.

Make sure the room in which you meet is clean. Cleanliness invites the Spirit and reflects the honor we give to the Lord. Seat people where they can see the proceedings of the meeting and where they can feel they are participants.

Sometimes meetings are so large that this is not always possible, but where it is, do it.

If you are a president, these details can be delegated to someone else.

Conduct from an Agenda

An agenda is a written plan that helps you know what comes next in the meeting and helps you remember names of participants and other details. Everything that needs to be done should be included on the agenda. Be sure to thank briefly those who have participated or helped in any way, and acknowledge visitors. With the written information in front of you, you can be calm and assured in your manner of conducting.

Stand While Conducting

When appropriate, stand while conducting a meeting. A possible exception to conducting from a standing position might be when you are leading a small meeting such as an executive meeting, or an informal meeting such as a discussion group. These are often held with all participants seated, sometimes around a table. But usually, unless you are physically unable to do so, you should stand to conduct most meetings.

Stand tall and straight, squarely on both feet, without shifting your weight from one foot to the other. This is pleasing to look at and helps convey a sense of dignity and assurance. It also gives you the freedom to turn and gesture comfortably and naturally.

Look at Those Who Are Present

Except for when you need to glance at notes, avoid looking down at the table or pulpit. And don't gaze up at the ceiling or at the back wall! To lend dignity to the occasion and to be able to convey warmth and openness, you need to be able to meet the eyes of those who are in the meeting. This will also help you drive home the ideas or information that you will be expressing.

Speak with Energy in a Voice All Can Hear

Let your natural voice inflections flow. Avoid speaking too fast, although speaking too slowly does tend to allow minds to wander and puts some listeners to sleep. Do your best to vary the pace, volume, and pitch of your voice so that you can engage the interest of listeners and help them understand what you are saying.

Be Courteous and Kind to All Present

Efficiency does not excuse lack of kindness and courtesy. I must admit that sometimes leaders—and I am no exception—become so anxious or focused on the purposes of a meeting that they seem abrupt or rushed. Try to avoid harshness in everything you do. In meetings use the terms *Brother* and *Sister* when referring to individuals, even if you are referring to your personal friends. This shows respect and contributes dignity to the meeting. Acknowledge visitors and make introductions when needed.

Be Attentive to Guest Speakers or Authorities

I was concerned at one stake conference to observe that a member of the Quorum of the Twelve Apostles was left on his own to find his way through the crowd of people to the podium. He introduced himself to those he passed and those on the stand until members of the stake presidency appeared.

Of course, he was perfectly capable of taking care of himself. But in my opinion, a General Authority who is a guest in a meeting should be shown honor and respect by having someone attend him and introduce him to members. His personal safety is another important consideration. You may never host a general officer of the Church, but your local priesthood advisers and stake officers deserve the same kind of consideration.

Now, a confession: I recently conducted our ward Christmas party, at which our stake president and his wife were present. With all the conducting I have done, and even though I know better, I inadvertently neglected to acknowledge and introduce them. I am still red-faced about it! It won't happen again.

I have always been most graciously attended whenever I have visited a stake or region of the Church. It is a comfortable feeling to have a stake officer leading me through a building, pointing out the location of drinking fountains and rest rooms, showing me a secure place for my personal belongings, and reviewing the preparations that have been made for the meeting. I have also appreciated a glass of water and a box of tissues at the pulpit.

Plan for the Unexpected

Some people say that whatever can go wrong in a meeting probably will. That's a bit too pessimistic for me, but a wise leader will anticipate what might happen. The unexpected could be anything—a storm that delays attendees, a larger crowd than expected, an interruption of electrical power, a guest speaker who is late, or an organist who calls in sick at the last minute.

Former Primary general president Dwan Young often counseled Primary leaders to have a plan B to use when plan A didn't work. In Primary this means you need to have a surprise attention-getter if the children's attention wanders, or a backup teacher always on deck, or a fill-in Sharing Time you seemingly pull out of the air.

Several years ago in a Relief Society meeting, I noticed the presidency was a little anxious during our opening song and announcements. A counselor left the room and returned a few minutes later. They kept watching the door. Finally, the time for the lesson arrived and the president announced that the teacher wasn't there. They had called her home but found that no one answered. They hoped she would walk in any second. We waited a few minutes. We sang an extra song to fill a few moments. The presidency whispered with each other. The president finally stood and said, "It appears that she isn't coming, and we'd like to ask Sister Dabb to give the lesson." Sister Dabb did an admirable job, based on a lifetime of study and preparation. Weren't they lucky to have a backup teacher? What great insurance!

Sometimes the projector bulb burns out, someone gets sick, or the door to the meetinghouse is locked. What kinds of plan Bs would you make to meet those situations? A few minutes preparing for the unexpected can substantially reduce anxiety on the part of a leader and often prevents problems before they occur.

Now, when you conduct a meeting the best you can and it doesn't turn out the way you had hoped, don't despair. Even if you feel it was all your fault—and it probably wasn't—just remember: Tomorrow is another day, and Heavenly Father still loves you. (I just hope our stake president forgives me!) Everyone makes mistakes in conducting sometimes. Emergencies happen that are beyond our control. Handling them with confidence and poise is all that is necessary. A little humor might help too.

Have confidence in your conducting of meetings, allow for and forgive your mistakes and the mistakes of others, try to do better each time, and know that when you have done your best, the Lord accepts your offering.

CHAPTER FOURTEEN

A Word to the Men

A woman that feareth the Lord,
she shall be praised.
—Proverbs 31:30

This chapter is one woman's point of view on the kinds of support women leaders need from men. Addressed to husbands of women who serve in Church callings and to priesthood leaders who advise the auxiliary organizations, it is based on my nearly twenty years of meeting with and listening to the thoughts and feelings of hundreds of women all over the Church.

A woman leader has probably given you this chapter to read and may have written her own ideas in the blank spaces. I hope reading this chapter will open the way for conversations about reciprocal support. With your wife or with the women you advise, you could discuss questions such as: How can I help you more effectively? What kind of support do you need? How can I fulfill my calling better? Such discussions can lead to increasing effectiveness as you strive to learn and grow in your callings.

To the Husband

You are a vital influence on how your wife executes her responsibilities in her Church calling. Her attitudes and effectiveness are greatly influenced by what she perceives your attitudes to be and what you do to support her.

Here are some ideas for you to consider:

Make It Easy for Her to Serve

Your wife has accepted a calling from the Lord to help others know and live the gospel. Her calling is a way for her to show her love for the Lord and for her to serve Church members. It is also an opportunity for her to grow spiritually, to grow in ability, and to develop her talents. Her growth has the potential to enrich your marriage and your family relationships. So anything you can do to make serving in the Church easy for her is likely to be returned to you in the form of many blessings.

You can make it easy for her by:

—Refraining from grumbling or complaining when she needs to attend meetings or when she needs to prepare
—Asking her if she needs time for her duties
—Asking what you can do to help
—Offering to watch the children or prepare a meal

_____

_____

_____

Encourage Her

Sometimes your wife may be discouraged and feel overwhelmed by her responsibilities. You can be a source of strength and encouragement to her by:

—Regularly reading the scriptures together
—Praying together

—Giving her a priesthood blessing when needed
—Reminding her of past successes

_____
_____
_____

Listen to Her

You may be tempted to tell your wife what she is doing wrong and how she can do better. This is a natural response when you care about someone and want to help them. However, it may be better for you to refrain from giving advice unless she asks. You might want to let her know you are willing to make suggestions if she would like them, but she mostly needs to feel that you love her, understand her, and support her.

You can listen in a way that will show support by:

—Stopping what you arc doing and looking at her
—Asking questions to clarify what she says
—Resisting the urge to preach
—Helping deflect interruptions by others
—Not letting her tears upset or frustrate you

_____
_____
_____

During the time I was Primary general president, often someone would say something like, "I think it's so wonderful that your husband lets you do all this." My response was usually something like, *"Lets* me? He *makes* me!" We'd laugh and then I would explain how supportive he is.

For example, he always encouraged me to do what I needed to do. One year when I was a counselor I had two international training assignments within six months. Our youngest daughter was just eleven at the time, and I was concerned about leaving. Leonard assured me that everyone would be fine. And they were.

He made it fun for the children when I was gone. Eating out, staying up watching videos, playing games, and generally goofing off were not unusual. I'm not sure that is the best way to compensate for Mother's absence, but that's how it was at our house.

After that year with two extended absences from home, I requested that I not travel internationally the following year. When Leonard found out I had done that, he said I should not hold back or restrict my Primary work in any way, because our children and he would be all right. He felt I should give my all.

Once the children were grown and gone from home, he worked on household projects when I was away for more than a day—just to surprise me. He painted, he installed new carpet, and once he even remodeled the bathroom! It got so I could hardly wait to get back home to see what he had done. When I would walk in the door, he'd wait for me to discover what was new and exclaim over it.

But more important was his supportive attitude—encouraging me, telling me I could do it, listening endlessly to my talks, preparing his own supper, and generally pampering me. It was just what I needed.

To the Priesthood Leader

You may be interested in a woman's commentary on how bishopric, high council, and stake presidency advisers to auxiliaries can be supportive of women leaders. This information will be helpful to you as you meet, work, and counsel with the women who serve in the presidencies and other organizations in your stake or ward. The ideas here are based on the premise that you have studied the organization's handbook and understand the purposes and goals stated therein, as well as the specific responsibilities you have been given to assist in accomplishing those purposes.

Here are some ideas for you to consider:

Give Effective Calls

Elder Jack L. Goaslind has said, "Calling someone to serve . . . is an act of love, offering them an opportunity for greater spiritual growth. Ensure them they are needed and valued. Help them succeed." ("Teacher, Do You Love Me?" Primary leaders fireside, 1986.)

You can offer women this opportunity for spiritual growth during a call when you:

—Express your commitment to the gospel of Jesus Christ
—Let her know the importance of her new calling
—Tell her with whom she will be serving
—Use the appropriate handbook to give her a good idea of what her duties will be
—Express your confidence in her

_____
_____
_____

Meet Regularly with Presidencies and Other Designated Leaders

This is your opportunity to learn more about what is happening to the members in their organizations, and to help the presidency learn how to be leaders.

In your meetings you could:

—Discuss ward and/or stake goals
—Ask for the leaders' ideas for achieving goals
—Share your feelings about what needs to be done
—Help them learn how to be leaders
—Provide them with information they need
—Hear their concerns
—Express your views
—Give counsel as needed

_____

_____

_____

Listen

Women leaders are able to observe and understand some things with a view that is different from yours. They may have information you need. It would be helpful to you to listen to them before you make decisions or take action. If you jump to a conclusion before they are finished talking, you may take action on a matter without full information. In addition, if you do not listen, women may feel that they have not been understood.

Listening can be helpful when you:

—Are patient and attentive
—Try to understand how they feel
—Ask what they would like you to do

_____

_____

_____

Act Expeditiously

To avoid causing frustration to auxiliary leaders, act quickly on matters concerning their organization. Some matters of decision can wait until your next meeting. However, sometimes a few brief but productive phone calls can provide the women with an answer they need to move ahead.

You can take action by:

—Filling staffing vacancies promptly
—Answering questions without delay
—Acknowledging phone calls and written communications

_____

_____

_____

Visit the Auxiliary Meeting When Needed

You are busy and have much demanded of you. But when you can, attend an auxiliary meeting and observe, and you will learn much.

You can make auxiliary visits meaningful if you:

—Observe carefully what is happening
—Give a short inspirational message to members

_____

_____

_____

I received a heartening and most welcome letter from a counselor in a stake Primary presidency regarding the member of the bishopric who advised the Primary in her ward. She wrote, "When I was in the Primary presidency in our ward, our priesthood leader was super and we appreciated him. This brother would often attend our meetings. Just his presence gave us confidence and courage to meet every problem. He would meet with the presidency monthly, kneeling in prayer with us, and then discuss every Primary worker and child, expressing great love and concern. He attended every leadership meeting. . . . He always had an inspirational and teaching message. He visited classes and gave counsel to problem children. I cannot think of one thing more this brother could have done to aid us in having a successful Primary. We had virtually no turnover in teachers, very few last-minute substitutes, high attendance and activation, and almost 100 percent attendance at ward and stake leadership meetings. This man had great influence on our Primary."

She described an equally effective high council adviser to their stake Primary presidency. Leaders like these men cannot imagine the strength and benefit they give to their auxiliary leaders and members.

Brethren, this book has been addressed mostly to women, and I have filled it with ideas that can help them be better leaders. I assure you that I have included ways they can understand and work effectively and in harmony with the men they live with and with whom they associate in the Church.

But they cannot do it alone.

The Church of Jesus Christ of Latter-day Saints provides fertile ground where seedlings of individual talents can be cherished and nurtured in a climate of unity, resulting in a harvest of greater love and individual and collective spiritual growth. You are vital to establishing such a climate where all can enjoy that harvest to the fullest. I pray that you might have the desire, vision, and blessings you need to make it so.

The Last Word:
Serving Others—
Good for What Ails You!

I was in a Primary General Board committee meeting when a secretary from our office entered the room and motioned to me to step out into the hall. When I did so, she handed me a note that had a Church office extension number on it. Now, as a board member, I was not accustomed to having the secretaries summon me, nor was it usual for me to be requested to call someone in Church headquarters. My husband had occasionally had business in what was then the building department, so I thought maybe he was in the office building calling for me.

The secretary had recognized the extension number. Curious, she stood right by me as I made the call. As the voice on the other end answered, my eyes widened and I mouthed silently, "The *First Presidency's* office!"

Brother D. Arthur Haycock, then secretary to the First Presidency, came on the line and greeted me, "Good afternoon, Sister Grassli. How are you?"

What a question! At that moment I didn't even know my name, much less how I was.

Brother Haycock told me that President Spencer W. Kimball wished to meet with me. He gave me instructions as to how to find the office, since I had not been in the administration building where most General Authority offices are located.

My heart pounded as I made my way to the administration building. I couldn't imagine why I had been summoned. I was the youngest, least experienced, least talented, and least visible or vocal of the board members. What could President Kimball possibly want?

With knees shaking, I thought of the dress I had put on that morning in a rush to leave the house. After I had dressed, I had remembered why I hadn't worn it for a while. It was old and had a small hole near the hem, burned by a cinder that had popped from the fireplace one day as I was standing near it. *Oh well,* I had said to myself. *I'm late. It's just a committee meeting. Nobody will notice it.* Now I was sorry I had not stopped to change. *It's not worthy of an audience with a prophet,* I thought.

As Brother Haycock ushered me into President Kimball's office, I was enveloped by a feeling of calm peace. We were introduced, President Kimball shook my hand warmly, and I sat down in a chair across the desk from the prophet. He didn't even look at the dress I was wearing. Silly me.

"Sister Grassli, today we've called Sister Dwan Young to be the new Primary president and Sister Virginia Cannon to be the new first counselor. We'd like you to serve as the second counselor."

I was speechless. He waited. I could hardly breathe.

"Sister Grassli?" Pause. "Do you feel you can accept the call, Sister Grassli?"

"Yes. Yes, of course, President Kimball." I couldn't imagine how I could do it, but I was not accustomed to declining a call to serve.

Then there was an especially long pause. I didn't know what to do next. President Kimball looked at me. I looked back. He looked some more. I started to get uneasy. My thoughts turned to my inadequacies, faults, and failings—all the reasons why I thought I was not a good choice for the call. As these thoughts played out in my head, I remembered hearing that prophets can see things sometimes that others cannot. I thought, *He's seeing my imperfections!* As President Kimball continued to sit silently, I was sure he was scrutinizing me.

Then suddenly the thought popped into my mind, *Oh! He's sorry already!*

Thinking—erroneously, of course—that a prophet needed an invitation to call someone to repentance, I asked, "President Kimball, do you have any counsel for me?"

"Well, yes, I do."

This is it, I thought.

But he didn't call me to repentance. He said simply, "Find joy in the service of God."

And I have since done just that. It has been challenging and stretching and frightening and fulfilling. I have seen faces of every age, size, color, and culture. I have sung hymns in many languages. I have made friends around the world. Men and women with whom I have served will be dear to me forever. I have been blessed and privileged to meet with prophets. But most rewarding is the realization that the gospel is true and brings blessings to many lives, including our family. And few things have been more satisfying than teaching my Primary class of boys twenty-five years ago, or leading the singing in Relief Society, or asking members to sing in sacrament meeting, or helping youth prepare a road show.

When I am down, I think of the joy I experience through service, and I am renewed. It's good for what ails me!

Find joy in serving the Lord.

That is my last word.

P. S. I never wore the dress again.

Index